Few Americans have been so much a part of American public life—yet so much apart from it—as Eugene McCarthy. A former U.S. Congressman, a two-term Senator, and contender for the Presidency in 1968, he is a keen-sighted observer of our political landscape, with a near-ideal mix of detachment and commitment at his command. McCarthy's essays and articles span the decade. They are informed with seamless intelligence throughout and laced with cunning Irish wit.

McCarthy articulates American politics and government with equal parts entertainment, analysis, revelation, and irony. A senior statesman, author, poet, teacher, orator, and the dethroner of a President—McCarthy wears all his hats here, from the wry "Musical Wars" to the deadly serious "Look, No Allies."

Those who savor the well-wrought essay and all those who heed the trends in U.S. politics, history, and government will find this pungent and pleasurable reading.

REQUIRED READING

REQUIRED READING

A DECADE OF POLITICAL
WIT & WISDOM

EUGENE McCARTHY

Harcourt Brace Jovanovich, Publishers

SAN DIEGO   NEW YORK   LONDON

*The lines from the poem "New Hampshire" by Robert Frost,
quoted in "Ten Things a Candidate
Should Know About New Hampshire,"
is from* The Poetry of Robert Frost, *edited
by E. C. Lathem. Copyright © 1923,
© 1969 by Holt Rinehart and Winston.
Copyright © 1951 by Robert Frost. Reprinted
by permission.*

Library of Congress Cataloging-in-Publication Data

*McCarthy, Eugene J., 1916–
Required reading: a decade of political wit and wisdom/E.
McCarthy.—1st ed.
p. cm.
Includes index.
ISBN 0-15-176880-3
1. United States—Politics and government—1981– 2. Presidents—
United States—Election—1988. I. Title.*
E.876.M39 1988
973.92—dc19   88-16448

Printed in the United States of America

First edition

A B C D E

Contents

PART I

OF CANDIDATES AND CAMPAIGNS

PART II

OF SUBSTANCE—SENSE AND NONSENSE

PART III

OF MEDIA, MESSAGES, AND MISCELLANEOUS

Contents

FOREWORD

This book is a selection rather than a collection of essays. Possibly it would be better described as a collection of selections. The standard by which inclusion was determined was not quite a "principle," but more a general determination that each essay had some relevance to the politics of 1988; in some cases, direct and immediate bearing on both politics and the operating government; in others, indirect and more removed, but never irrelevant.

The more thoughtful ones have, as theme and substance, the Constitution of the United States and the underlying principles of democratic government and society. Others deal with the application of these principles, and with current matters of politics and of government. A few, incidentally and almost by inadvertence, touch on personalities.

Some of these essays were printed in the right places at the right time. Some have been heeded, others ignored and appear here as second comings, not wholly out of place or time. Some were rejected absolutely and finally; *The Wall Street Journal*, the *New York Times*, and the *Washington Post* were the most frequent offenders. A good number were saved from slow death—abandoned in draft and languishing in drawers and filing cabinets—by the *Culpeper* or *Rappahannock News*, or by the *Rushville* [Indiana] *Republican*. Some have been rewritten for this publication. Others are wholly new.

It is the opinion of the editors as well as the view of the author that not more than three of the essays in the book should be read in any one day, with one essay being selected from each of the book's three divisions. It is also the opinion of the same persons that those who read and meditate upon these texts in an election year will be better informed than other citizens of the country.

———*E.M.*
APRIL 1988

Part I

OF CANDIDATES AND CAMPAIGNS

TEN THINGS A CANDIDATE
SHOULD KNOW ABOUT
NEW HAMPSHIRE

(New York Times Magazine, December 30, 1979)

The New Hampshire primary is a high-risk venture for presidential candidates. More lose there, in fact, than win. But the important thing, in the first primary of the campaign season, is to beat the polls, not the opponents. A candidate can win the New Hampshire primary and not be nominated by his party—as was the case with Estes Kefauver in 1952 and in 1956, and with Henry Cabot Lodge in 1964; or lose the primary and be nominated by his party—as Barry Goldwater was in 1964.

On the other hand, he can win in New Hampshire and be declared the loser by the press and political pundits, as happened to

Edmund Muskie in 1972. (Although Senator Muskie received 46 percent of the vote—9 percent more than George McGovern—the press had decided that if he didn't get 65 percent, he would lose the election.)

Or a candidate can lose the primary and be declared the winner, which happened to Senator McGovern. Early in the campaign, a Gallup poll had predicted he would receive only 3 percent of the vote, but because his percentage was approximately twelve times that, the media decided that he had won.

I had been slated to receive 12 percent, 18 percent, and between 25 and 28 percent of the primary vote in three different pre-New Hampshire polls in 1968. So, although President Lyndon Johnson received about 49 percent of the Democratic vote and I received 42.4 percent, I was credited with having defeated him in the March 12 primary. As a survivor of that primary, I believe my insights might be of some assistance to those who will brave the cold—and sometimes ill—winds of New Hampshire. To help combat the uncertainties and apparent contradictions in the interpretations and consequences of the primaries themselves, here are ten tips to alert candidates to the many dangers along the campaign route.

1. New Hampshire is not a simple state. Like Gaul, it is divided into three parts: Massachusetts, Maine, and Vermont. In approaching New Hampshire for campaign purposes, a candidate must be aware that each of these states influences the economics of the towns directly across the border. In anticipation of campaigning in southeastern New Hampshire, a candidate should enter from Massachusetts. Southeastern New Hampshire is an extension of the old manufacturing and mill areas of its southern neighbor. On the Massachusetts side of the line are towns such as Lowell and Lynn and Lawrence; on the New Hampshire side, Manchester, Concord, and Dover. Industry seeking cheaper labor in the manufacturing of textiles and shoes has moved north across the line.

In 1968, one could scarcely tell when one had left Massachusetts and entered New Hampshire. North of the border, the towns looked slightly older; the abandoned mills, more abandoned. But the passage from state to state was marked by a particular set of distinguishing signs—those advertising chiropractors and chiropractic clinics. Major advertising by chiropractors, evidently, was banned in Massachusetts in 1968, but not across the border. New Hampshire was willing to have the business and was considerate of skiers in need of adjustments.

To campaign in northeastern New Hampshire, beyond the White Mountains, the candidate comes in from Maine. Here he will find forests of pine, balsam, cedar, and birch; a land of lakes, of pulpwood, and of paper mills with the smell of sulfur hanging over the towns. The inhabitants are either what are called "native whites"—with Anglo-Saxon names—or French Canadians. Wood and the woods are their livelihood. In winter, the campaign season, these persons are generally silent, purposeful, and committed; their standard clothing is a plaid shirt worn under a padded blue jacket and a red cap. These New Hampshire persons pay little attention to visitors, even candidates, and would as soon not shake hands if the act requires removal of gloves or chopping mittens.

Then there is western New Hampshire, which should be entered from Vermont. It is a land of high hills—mountains, some of them—of sheltered farms, and of near-perfect towns and villages: Peterborough, Claremont, Lebanon, Franconia, Antrim, Bungy, and Still Corners. The struggle for survival in this part of New Hampshire is real in the winter, but somehow it seems in better balance than it is in the southeast or in the north. Wood smoke is reassuring as it rises from the farmhouses and settles over the towns.

Anyone who campaigns in Keene should be familiar with the case for the admission of Smokey Joe Woods to the

Cooperstown, New York, Baseball Hall of Fame. A great in-
justice has been done to Smokey Joe. He might have qualified either as a pitcher or as the hitting outfielder he was
when his arm failed, except for the fact that his two separate careers were too short to qualify him. Projecting his
pitching record forward would have placed him on a par
with his contemporary, Walter Johnson, and slightly above
Sandy Koufax. Projecting his hitting record back over the
years during which he was pitching would have ranked him
with the best hitters on record.

One final thing a candidate should be aware of is that
each New England state looks upon animals differently.
As John Ciardi points out in his poem about the porcu-
pine:

Vermont pays a bounty on his nose;
New Hampshire on his ears . . .
And Maine has seen fit to protect him as the one

Edible, substantial and common meat
A man lost in the woods can kill readily
With nothing but rocks and a club. *

2. No matter when or how a candidate enters New
Hampshire, he will either be met or soon found out by the
Manchester *Union Leader* and its well-known publisher,
William Loeb. * *

Any candidate not favored by Loeb had better keep his
guard up. The target of his paper in 1980 was Philip
Crane, a conservative Republican who entered New
Hampshire to challenge Ronald Reagan, Loeb's choice.
Crane was met by editorial attacks charging him with
sexual excesses.

---

* By permission of the author.
* * Mr. Loeb is since deceased.

Senator Muskie, the victim of the famous "Canuck" letter and of printed attacks on his wife, was induced to challenge Loeb from a truck bed parked outside the *Union Leader*'s office before the 1972 primary. During his attack—or counterattack—on Loeb, Senator Muskie was reported to have been "visibly moved," perhaps to the point of tears.

In 1968, Loeb referred to me as "a skunk," and printed a letter to the editor in which it was charged that while the oath of allegiance to the flag was being taken, preceding a speech I was to give at a high-school assembly, my lips did not move.

Every candidate should, in anticipation of entering the New Hampshire primary, subscribe to the *Union Leader* for a month or two, in order to develop understanding and respect for the persons who read it day after day. Then he should decide either to surrender to its editorials or stand against them.

3. Candidates should not enter New Hampshire too early. Visitors to the state in early fall are tolerated as leaf viewers. But in October and November, New Hampshire residents do not wish to be distracted from their work of getting ready for winter. They are cutting, splitting, and piling wood. They are putting up storm windows and storm doors and covering screened and open porches with plastic. Some are putting tar paper around stone foundations, and banking houses with straw, or with banking material of an older tradition: barnyard manure, which will, through the winter, generate modest heat.

Political thinking in New Hampshire in presidential years is reserved principally for January and February. It ends when the sap begins to rise in the maple trees. The state resents the efforts of other states and of political parties to encroach on its claim to the earliest primary in the nation.

In 1972, Florida moved its primary date up to the second Tuesday in March, the same date as that of the New Hampshire primary. New Hampshire promptly moved its primary to the first Tuesday in March. In 1976, Massachusetts and Vermont decided to hold their primaries on the first Tuesday in March. New Hampshire immediately moved its primary to the last Tuesday in February. New Hampshire likes to make its presidential decisions in a time when there are no distractions except those essential to survival.

4. Primary candidates should keep in mind that New Hampshire is a modest state, that it lives carefully, not trusting anyone with too much power. Although one of the smallest states in the Union, it has the largest legislative body. Candidates who promise too much are not likely to do well there.

Law-and-order is a compelling issue in this New England state, which has a very low crime rate. In 1976, it had only 248 men and no women in federal and state prisons. Maine had ten women in prison, and Vermont had six.

New Hampshire finances its government with taxes on the vices of its own people, but even more so on the vices and near-vices of visitors from other states. It taxes tobacco and betting on horses. It taxes hotel and motel rooms and restaurant meals, and it runs a state-administered lottery.

Skiing is for outsiders, ice hockey for natives. If, in anticipation of his campaign, John Connally did, as reported, buy a ski lodge, he made a mistake. He should have bought—or, better, built—a skating and ice-hockey arena.

Connally's public purchase of snow-country boots was also a mistake—it may have been a manifestation of his Texas preoccupation with boots. One presidential candidate, George Romney, was last seen, politically, wearing winterwear with boots in New Hampshire in 1968. Ordinary shoes, with rubbers, are the approved footwear for candidates.

5. New Hampshire is restrained in its claim to distinction. The *Information Please Almanac*, which all potential candidates for the New Hampshire primary should read, lists fruit and potatoes among its principal crops but makes no special claim as to quality or numbers. Maine, by contrast, asserts in the *Almanac* that it produces one out of every nine potatoes raised in the United States, and nineteen out of every twenty blueberries, to say nothing of 100 million canned sardines. Massachusetts is, according to the book, a leading manufacturer of electronic equipment, and it boasts of having one of the largest Irish populations in the nation. New Hampshire, on the other hand, simply states that it manufactures electrical goods and produces machinery, leather goods, textiles, and paper products.

It also produces maple syrup and maple sugar, and it is called the Granite State. But Vermont, according to the *Almanac*, leads all states of the Union in the production of both maple syrup and granite.

The state tree of Massachusetts is the American elm; that of Maine, the white pine; New Hampshire's state tree is the unassuming, modest, scarcely useful birch—without an adjective.

New Hampshire does claim to have the highest mountain in the Northeast, Mount Washington—among the lowest mountains in the country.

6. Candidates must visit factories. In going through shoe and textile plants, they should be mindful of the observation of the poet Robert Lowell that, despite pay and working conditions, workers in shoe factories are happier than those working in textiles and clothing. Five thousand

pairs of shoes without feet or legs lined up on a rack are
quite purposeful and look confident, Lowell noted, "as
though destined to belong to someone." Five hundred
sweaters in a flat pile give no hint as to the person who
may own or wear them.

7. With energy a central issue, it will be especially important for candidates to be well informed about wood and
wood-burning stoves.

The relative heating power of the principal types of fire-
wood should be known. Giving actual Btu measurements
may be a little too much, but such measurements are
available. For example, there are approximately 18 million
Btu's per cord of white ash, and only about 11 million
Btu's per cord of quaking aspen. Thus, a candidate should
be able to identify and classify major categories of wood—
such as oak, hickory, ash, and sugar maple for heat and
steady fire; red maple, elm, and box elder for light and
easy burning; pine and apple for smell. And, to be dis-
dained, willow, poplar, gum, and basswood. He should
know a potbellied stove from a box stove, an Olympic par-
lor stove, Fisher and Shenandoah models, Bucks and Rite-
ways, and foreign makes such as the Norwegian Jøtuls and
the Danish Langes.

A candidate should know what a nonhydraulic splitter
is, and what the differences are among a splitting maul, a
single-bit chopper ax with a head and poll, and a double-
bit ax. He should recognize a "fawn foot" ax handle as
well as one with a "swell knob," and know that all good
ax handles (helves) are made from second-growth hickory.

If, on a visit to a sawmill, the candidate really wishes to
show off, he might ask who "hammers" the circular saw
when it loses its temper.

8. New Hampshire is not for sale, nor does it seek approval, as Robert Frost has written in a poem called "New
Hampshire":

Just specimens is all
  New Hampshire has,
One each of everything
  as in a showcase,
Which naturally she
  doesn't care to sell. . . .
She's one of the two best
  states in the Union.
Vermont's the other. . . .

9. Remember that a good winter driver experienced in ice and snow is much more important in New Hampshire than a good advance man or press secretary.

10. Finally, if, as a candidate, you think you feel a groundswell, be careful. It may be no more nor less than a frost heave.

FROM PLAGIARISM TO PLAGIAT

(1988)

Plagiarism has been an issue in the 1987–88 presidential campaign. The issue first surfaced in a relatively simple and innocuous form early this year when a joke used by Senator Albert Gore was claimed by or for Congressman Mo Udall. The congressman has a well-deserved reputation as a wit and storyteller. Having collected jokes for years (Abraham Lincoln is reported to have done the same), Gore recently published a book of copyrighted jokes and stories. Whether jokes can be copyrighted remains an unsettled legal question.

In any case, no charge of violation of copyright was made against

Senator Gore. The matter in contention was the story of the candidate who comes into a store, or barbershop, and announces that he is a candidate for president of the United States, whereupon someone in the group says, "Yes, we were laughing about that this morning." Senator Gore's defense was that he had changed both the time and the place of the Udall story. The charge was not pushed very hard or far either by the press or by Congressman Udall, or by his supporters and admirers. Using someone else's joke is marginal plagiarism and scarcely deserving of the label.

Jokes do not long remain the property of their originators. If the author of a joke is credited publicly more than once or twice, he or she has probably received as much credit as may be expected. Moreover, good basic jokes are more or less standardized, universal, and timeless. To claim authorship is dangerous. Some scholar or journalist may remember, or with the assistance of a data bank and computer discover, that the joke (or something very close to it) has long been in circulation, possibly for centuries. In the midst of a drive against sending pornographic materials through the mails, Postmaster General Arthur Summerfield, of the Eisenhower administration, took *Lysistrata* off the list of banned books when he learned it was 2,000-year-old pornography.

The second case of plagiarism in the campaign was more serious in substance and consequences. It brought about the withdrawal of Senator Joseph Biden from the presidential race. It also cast a pall over the candidacy of Governor Michael Dukakis of Massachusetts, whose campaign aides discovered and indirectly made public that in some of his speeches Senator Biden was using, without attribution, speeches or parts of speeches of other politicians, most notably Robert Kennedy, Hubert Humphrey, and Neil Kinnock, leader of the British Labour party. That the case became a critical one is somewhat surprising, since the attitude toward plagiarism by politicians in general is one of tolerance. The use of ghostwritten work is accepted. It is not demanded that phrases, possibly a line or two from literature or from someone else's speeches, be identified. Standardized speeches, those approaching GI-issue character, may be given by several party speakers without fear of being charged with plagiarism. Much of Senator Joseph McCarthy's well-known Wheeling, West Virginia, speech was taken from a speech given by Richard Nixon several weeks earlier. And several years ago, Senator Ted Kennedy was not judged severely when CBS discovered and reported that a speech he made had been given earlier by his brother Robert. Family plagiarism is acceptable, it seems.

Outside politics, judgment on plagiarists and plagiarism is not all harsh. Both Homer and Virgil were identified as plagiarists, but evidently with the approval of contemporaries, especially of lesser writers whose words or lines were included in the epic works of the masters. To be overlooked by Homer was considered serious enough to draw the comment of one critic who said that the works of Tiresias were so good that "they were worthy to be plagiarized by Homer." Today, lesser poets do not object to being included in the writings of Ezra Pound or T. S. Eliot. In his critical essays, Benjamin Jowett charges that Plato's works "are full of plagiarisms, inappropriately borrowed." Theologians, both ancient and modern, have been accused of borrowing ideas. The best, or certainly one of the best, riposte in such a case was made by a moral theologian, a monsignor in Minnesota. On being accused by a nun of lifting not one page but whole sections from the works of other theologians and including them in his book as his own, he replied, "Thank you very much. You are very perceptive, Sister. Would you care to join me in writing my next book?"

Medieval chroniclers were said to be "great plagiarists." Ben Jonson, possibly smarting a little because of Shakespeare's success with plagiarism, wrote in *The Poetaster*: "Why, the ditty is all borrowed: 'tis Horace's. Hang him for plagiary." And in our own time, the poet Robert Lowell, on being accused of using private letters as parts of poems, replied, "I improved them before using them."

With such variable and widely tolerant attitudes toward plagiarism, both in the political order and outside it, one must ask why such harsh judgment was passed on Senator Biden. I think there were three substantial reasons. First, he plagiarized from those in the political order who were not his inferiors or peers, but rather his superiors, unaware or indifferent to the guiding principle stated in *Blackwood's* magazine in 1863:

> Little wits that plagiarize
> Are but pick pockets;
> Great wits that plagiarize
> Are conquerors.

Second, he borrowed materials that were not wholly original. He plagiarized ghostwritten material, and some of it, in turn, contained plagiarized writing. He is guilty of a kind of compounded plagiarism—"not just plagiarizing," as the press said, "but committing plagiarism"—an action comparable to committing sin or even murder. He left himself open to the risk that a surviving ghostwriter (in this case, Adam Walinsky) would surface like a surrogate mother and claim credit for the original text.

Third, and finally, the Senator went beyond accepted political limits in plagiarizing Welsh politician Neil Kinnock's ideas and words, which in another realm of behavior may be roughly comparable to transporting persons across state lines under the Mann Act. More serious than taking Kinnock's ideas and words, Senator Biden also adopted a part of Neil Kinnock's life. In a figurative way, he became guilty of another form of plagiarism. Since the seventeenth century this form has been defined as "man stealing," and was last noted in United States history by John Adams. At the turn of the nineteenth century, he asserted that the impressment of American seamen by the British was "no better than what civilians call 'plagiat,' a crime punishable with death by all civilized nations."

STANDARDS AND GUIDES FOR

PICKING PRESIDENTIAL

CANDIDATES

(Adapted from *New Republic*, FEBRUARY 22, 1988)

Until 1960, the presidential selection process was reasonably structured, if not standardized. Party rules were generally consistent from one election to another and seldom changed. Radio and the written word were the principal means for communicating political ideas and the views of the candidates.

Two changes occurred in the 1960 campaign that altered the politics of future campaigns. John Kennedy's victories in primaries established the base upon which he secured the nomination, and his acknowledged success over Richard Nixon in the televised debate of that year established television as a major instrument and force in presidential politics. In subsequent campaigns, primaries have taken on new importance and have proliferated. More money is spent on television than on any other means of political communication.

In consequence, the selection of presidential candidates and the election of a president have come to be based, or at least strongly influenced by, considerations other than basic qualifications for the office. Primaries enable candidates to circumvent or overcome party controls. Television emphasizes the importance of criteria such as a candidate's appearance and projection of personality. Makeup persons become as important as speech writers, while the presidential selection process moves closer to a state of entropy: disorder, randomness, and chaos.

Since there is little evidence that the procedures are likely to become more orderly or rational before the next presidential election, it is important that individual voters simplify the process for themselves, establishing standards that may reduce the limits of chaos. Here are some suggestions that may be helpful. Persons in the following categories should be automatically, or categorically, rejected.

1. Governors or former governors, unless they have had experience with the federal government, either before or after their governorships. Governors in the presidency are overconfident. They are inclined to believe that they can balance the federal budget if they have balanced a state budget; that they can handle the Pentagon because they have sent out the National Guard to suppress student protest or control a strike; that they understand federal bureaucracies, such as the Internal Revenue Service, because they have reorganized a state highway department.

2. Vice presidents or former vice presidents. First, because they are too often put on the ticket for political reasons, rather than for their potential to be president. Second, because of the validity of the observation made by Senator

Paul Laxalt while he was still a candidate for the Republican presidential nomination, that the office is likely to weaken and confuse character. Both government and politics would be well served if the vice presidency were eliminated, a proposition that was given serious thought in 1803.

3. Ministers, sons and daughters of clergymen, and even persons who let themselves be called "leading lay persons." Religious judgment and commitment is fundamentally different from that of the political-secular order. The medieval distinction between the First Estate (religious) and the Second and Third Estates (both secular and civil) was a useful one, anticipating Oswald Spengler's observation that in any society the basic struggle is between only two estates, the religious and the civil.

4. Generals and admirals, for obvious reasons: the differences in authority, command, and the use of power in the military from that exercised in civil democratic order.

5. Heads of major corporations, "CEOs," as they are generally identified, whose experience of power and its uses is essentially feudal rather than democratic. This is especially true of former heads of major automobile companies.

An early checkpoint for judging candidates is their announcement of candidacy.

1. A voter should be highly skeptical of any candidate who makes his or her announcement in February. If a candidate does, it is fair to assume that the decision was made in that month, or that the candidate is unaware of the danger of making decisions in February, a time that throughout history has been considered a bad time for decisions. Ancient civilizations reserved that month for worship of the dead and the gods of the underworld.

2. Be wary of announcements that include a spouse and

children, having them present on the platform or mountainside, or, in the worst case, with the family dog.

3. Caution is advised if a candidate claims to represent a generation or special demographic/sociological group, such as the "war generation" or the "baby boomers." A candidate might claim a right to govern on the basis of having been conceived during the great blackout of New York City, approximately a generation ago.

4. Question a candidate if he or she publicizes medical reports (unless the candidate is suffering from a physical or psychological disorder that might immediately or seriously affect service in the presidential office). Jimmy Carter's statement in 1976 that he was allergic to beer, cheese, and mold, and that he sometimes suffered from hemorrhoids, was a case of unnecessary if not indecent exposure, as was Walter Mondale's revelation that same year that he had a hernia.

5. A candidate is suspect if it is stated that he or she has wanted the presidency very much and from an early age— say, twelve or eighteen years. Anyone under fifty is suspect, especially since one should be "willing" to be president, rather than "want" it.

Voters should also look for more subtle signs of demagoguery, which may be part of a candidate's past or may emerge during the presidential campaign. There are at least five such signs that are worthy of attention.

1. Does the candidate reserve the first seats in the second-class section of an airplane, thus being in position to greet and be seen by the tourist or second-class passengers on boarding but also to slip through the curtain to work the first-class section and even be invited by airline personnel to move up?

2. Does the candidate now—or has he in a past cam-

paign—call himself, for example, William (Bill) or Robert (Bob) or Patrick/Patricia (Pat)? Or does the candidate, known previously as John III or IV, drop the III or IV for the campaign, thus in effect repudiating father, grandfather, and possibly great grandfather?

3. Is the candidate so heavily into physical fitness (e.g., jogging) that he reports his time for the mile or two-mile run, or for longer distances? In the presidential campaign, does the candidate walk or bicycle across a state? These actions are marginally acceptable in campaigns for governor, but not for the presidency or even the Senate.

4. Does the candidate cry easily and often in public? What brings on the crying? Does the candidate cry out of the inner corner of the eye, the outer, or straight down the center of the lower lid, as Bette Davis did? Or do the eyes just well up? These distinctions should be observed.

5. Does the candidate take credit for—or has he or she been credited with strength of character because of—a primitive experience, without protesting such attribution? Jimmy Carter was given a high mark by *Newsweek* in 1976 because he had used an outdoor toilet, and Senator Muskie had his character formed and strengthened early in life because he was bathed in a washtub. I have had both of these experiences without realizing what they have done for my character.

There is a final set of candidates' attributes, claims, and experiences that deserves some weighing by prospective voters, and it involves more subtle physical, psychological, and political distinctions.

The first, and possibly most important, is represented by the generally approving statement "He (or she) knows the numbers," a reputation carried by Robert McNamara and David Stockman. Second, offered as a credit as well, is the statement that "He (or she) makes no small mistakes," also an achievement attributed to Robert McNamara. The danger in both of the above statements is that potential critics, so taken by the numbers known, fail to consider the significance of what is being numbered, or are so intent on watching for small mistakes that the big mistakes are likely to go unchallenged and unnoticed until too late. Third is that a candidate should not have survived on artificially supplied oxygen for long periods of time, either in outer space or in a submarine, or possibly as a mountain climber or a scuba diver. Fourth is speed reading. President Carter reportedly took it up while he was president and reported at one point that his retention rate had improved by 50 percent. He did not report the base from which the improvement had taken place or what was not retained. As a rule, what can be read quickly should not be of much concern to a president, and what should be of concern should not be speed read, considering the possibility of limited retention. Fifth is that a presidential candidate should be checked to determine whether he or she knows the difference in the techniques used to drive cattle and hogs. A cattle drive is started very slowly, best accompanied by gentle singing (e.g., "Get along, little dogies"). But once the herd is started, the pace is slowly and subtly increased; as they approach the stockyard or corral, the cattle are all but stampeded and given no time for thought. This was the favorite, near-exclusive technique used by President Johnson, and it was especially evident in his handling of the Vietnam War.

Generally recognized as more intelligent than cows, hogs must be panicked into motion. They must be yelled at in Latin ("*Sui, sui*"). Once hogs are started, they must be allowed to slow down gradually so that they arrive at the desired point at a slow walk, and are moved to think they knew where they were going all the time. As a rule, the House of Representatives should be subjected to the cattle technique, and the Senate to the hog-driving method.

If all of this is too much, the potential voter can follow the more cynical rules for political participation and (1) pay no attention to what a candidate is or has been; (2) pay no attention to what a candidate says he or she will do if it is something that cannot be done (e.g., "making the mountain come to Mohammed"); (3) pay no attention to what a candidate says he or she will not do, if it is something that he or she couldn't do in any case, as when King Canute said, "I will not turn back the tide"; (4) pay little attention to what the candidates say they will do, if they could do it, unless the matter is of great importance; and (5) look especially to what a candidate says he or she will not do if it is something he or she could do (and might do), and is something the voter considers important. Application of this rule would have warranted a vote for Richard Nixon in 1968, if one believed that recognition of China was of paramount importance, and a vote for Ronald Reagan in 1980, if one believed that reductions in nuclear arms, together with a partial nuclear disarmament of Europe, was the pressing issue of the eighties.

And if the voter is in despair, or near it, he or she might follow the advice of the man in the gold breastplate under the old stone cross, as reported by William Butler Yeats:

> Stay at home and drink your beer
> And let your neighbor vote.

HAVE OFFICE, WILL TRAVEL

(1988)

Unlike the candidates for the presidency in 1984, most of whom announced travel plans following the election, this year's candidates have said little or nothing about travel. In 1984 the Democratic candidates were divided on most issues; one was for two small aircraft carriers, rather than for a single large one. Another favored mobile missiles, but not of the size of the controversial MX. One or more were for fixed missiles of varying sizes. One was for free trade, others for protective tariffs, or for protection of American industry and jobs by some other means. Some supported high-technology industry (which makes more workers unnecessary); others were for subsidies to employers who would hire more workers to compete with high technology. So the differences ran, as they do this year. But in 1984 all agreed that soon after the election they would go at least halfway to meet the Russians.

The going-places-even-before-being-sworn-in-as-president was started by Dwight Eisenhower in 1952, when he said that if elected he would go to Korea. He was, and he did go—after he was elected but before he was sworn in as president.

On the other hand, Lyndon Johnson, as president, said that he would meet with the North Vietnamese any time, on a neutral ship in a neutral sea. When he left office, he had not yet found the neutral ship in the neutral sea.

In 1972 candidate George McGovern was quoted as saying that he would crawl to Hanoi, if assured that peace would result. The offer was not well received by the American electorate.

In 1984 candidate Walter Mondale was the first to speak firmly of travel plans when he said that on being elected he would immediately get on the hot line to Moscow and offer to meet the head of the Soviet government in Geneva, Switzerland, to discuss disarmament and improved relations between the U.S. and the USSR. He added, as a special reason for electing him, that he knew where the right telephone was in the White House. This seemed reassuring unless one wondered whether President Reagan had moved the telephone, in which case Mr. Mondale, if elected, might have gone looking for the phone where it had been during the Carter administration. (Gary Hart also said that if elected he would go to Geneva, but he did not mention first making any telephone calls from the White House.)

John Glenn, an astro-traveler, might well have offered to meet the Russian leader in orbit, in the same manner that Russian and American astronauts had linked space vehicles. In that rarefied atmosphere, at that speed, and with the earth visible below, Glenn might have claimed that negotiations would be more fruitful than in Geneva, with its limited vistas.

Senator Alan Cranston, also a candidate in 1984, did not offer to travel, although he challenged his opponents for nomination to jog with him, or hike, carrying a backpack of fifty pounds. He might have made a similar offer to the head of the Soviet Union, with the televised meeting to take place on a neutral track in a neutral country.

Occasionally a president travels with a fixed and defined purpose, such as signing a treaty. But nearly all presidential travels since the end of the Truman administration have had no clear public purpose. Thus, President Eisenhower traveled without any defined diplomatic mission, as did President Kennedy when he went to West Germany. (Kennedy later said that a president needing the encouragement of crowd support should go to Germany.) President Johnson, President Nixon—and even President Gerald Ford during his short stint in the White House—made similar trips.

Why do they do it? Is it out of loneliness, frustration, need for public acclaim? Unappreciated at home, do they go to show that they are liked abroad? Perhaps. But the real impetus, I believe, is deeper.

In trying to understand this presidential need, I was driven to study animal behavior in the hope that I might find an explanation. Quite by accident, I found the answer in an article on kangaroos in the August 1977 *Scientific American*. The basic study of kangaroo behavior is the work of T. J. Dawson of the University of New South Wales, C. Richard Taylor of Harvard University, and Knut Schmidt-Nielsen of Duke University. The impetus for presidential travels must be essentially what these experts have discovered about the hopping habits of the kangaroo.

Kangaroos, of course, hop if they are frightened and seek to escape danger. They also hop in search of food and for other purposes. But as far as can be determined, they sometimes hop without any clear purpose.

The motivation for this undirected hopping is wholly internal. When the kangaroo is inactive, there is a gradual energy buildup in the tendons of its hind legs. When the energy buildup reaches a critical point, the kangaroo begins hopping. When it has relieved the tension in its tendons, the kangaroo settles down and again becomes pentapedal (five-footed), using its four feet and its tail for support and motion.

It is very frustrating for the kangaroo to be restrained from hopping when it is ready to go. The same is true of presidents.

This year's candidates, before they think of foreign travel, might well think of announcing that if elected they would first go to the Pentagon. They could, if admitted, check up on war plans, the new weapons systems that are on the drawing boards, the contingency plans for world domination, and any other things involving the military-industrial complex. They might even do so with the fall-back position that if not admitted, they would seek diplomatic representation, possibly of ambassadorial rank.

TEN GUIDES IN VOTING FOR
CANDIDATES FOR THE SENATE

(Culpeper News, October 14, 1982)

Issues and party identification are, of course, of some importance in choosing candidates for the U.S. Senate, but there are other considerations of equal, if not more, importance. There are positive standards for judging senatorial attitudes and performance. There are also negative standards that, if they are the mark of candidates or incumbents, should serve as a warning.

Do not vote for a candidate who

> • often quotes, as the sole authority in support of his or her position, dead politicians and asserts that he or she

knows with certainty what the dead person would do if
alive. General George Marshall, of World War II fame, was
announced as a supporter of the Vietnam War by one of its
defenders long after the general had died.

• lives off an inheritance set up for him or her by grandparents or great grandparents. One living on a fund set up
by his or her father is within tolerable range of acceptance.
But if both grandparents and great grandparents anticipated
that their progeny were not to be trusted with the family
inheritance even unto the fourth generation, there is small
reason to accept that the same progeny should be given any
part in handling a federal budget of some $800 billion.

• uses a spouse, or spouse and children, as an explanation
or an excuse for a vote, especially if the vote is to increase
congressional salaries.

• states that he or she was moved to run for office by
sudden inspiration, or below the age of fourteen, on visiting
Washington, D.C., as part of a Boy or Girl Scout group.

• is touted by someone—friend, newspaper editor, or columnist—as having the potential to be a vice president.

• regularly quotes from three of the following four docu-
ments: The Bible (all right if he or she gives only book and
author, but not chapter and verse); the Internal Revenue
Code, by title and subtitle, and finer distinctions; the
Summa Theologica of St. Thomas Aquinas, identifying
question and answer; the rules of the United States Senate
by title, chapter, and paragraph. (This strict rule applies
only to incumbents, but in a removed form can be applied
to any challenger who says that if elected he or she will
master the Senate rules.)

• uses the family dog as a defense against any charges
leveled against him or her, or is observed to change breeds
from one election to another so as to have in the family
picture a dog of the currently most popular breed. Defend-
ing one's dog from public attack is not only acceptable but

commendable, as in the case of Franklin Roosevelt's dog, Fala.

• publishes his or her income tax returns and challenges opponents to do the same—in most cases a case of indecent overexposure.

• promises that he or she will have a perfect attendance record for quorum calls and roll calls—a certain commitment to waste of time.

• says that he or she listens a lot to constituents, and subscribes to a "quotation service."

WE KILLED ST. GEORGE
AND KEPT THE DRAGON

(St. Louis Post-Dispatch, SEPTEMBER 2, 1984)

"The Puritans," wrote Gilbert Chesterton, "wind up killing St. George and keeping the dragon." So is it going with the federal election amendments of 1975–76 and their complement of reform laws and codes designed to purify politics and politicians. Geraldine Ferraro appears now to be the victim of these zealous efforts to ensure integrity in public office—efforts and actions that both she and the Democratic presidential nominee, Walter Mondale, supported.

The principal arguments made for the election control and financing laws were that money was the root of all political evil, a position strongly supported by Common Cause, and that the United States political system had been, or was being, corrupted by money, principally in the form of large contributions to campaign expenditures.

The arguments ignored the fact that the higher levels of political corruption come from the desire for power and pride in office, usually demonstrated as excessive concern about what "history may say" about a politician. If Richard Nixon was corrupted, it was not through money or large contributions, or the influence that large contributors may have had upon him. The contributions may have helped him in his drive for power and historical recognition, but they were not inherently corrupting. Nor is there evidence at levels of politics below the presidency that money has had a significant corrupting influence.

The evidence of corruption generally cited in presidential politics is usually what is called the "purchase of ambassadorships." It may be a questionable practice to award ambassadorships to large contributors, but the record does not show that politics or foreign policy has been corrupted over the years because of this practice.

Moreover, there is clear historical evidence that large contributors have been highly important in supporting controversial political movements, and in challenging established ideas, practices, and institutions. The American Revolution, for example, was not financed by small contributions or with matching funds from George III. It was financed at critical times by large contributions from persons such as Haym Salomon, John Hancock, and others, and even by contributions from foreigners whom we have long honored, such as the Marquis de Lafayette, whose help would be illegal under the existing reforms.

In any case, even though more serious corruption because of money could be demonstrated to exist, that fact would not justify the broad attack on political traditions and on constitutional guarantees that is basic to the 1975–76 campaign law, a law that violates—in some cases directly, in others indirectly—almost every personal and political right guaranteed by the Constitution. It limits freedom of speech. It gives special privileges and advantages to the two major parties—in effect, legalizing the Republican and the Democratic parties in a way similar to the violation of the Constitution that would be inherent in the legalization of two religions. I am sure that if the Founding Fathers had anticipated a time when one, two, or more political parties would be given formal support by the government, an additional amendment would have been included in the Bill of Rights, forbidding the establishment or support of political parties by the federal government.

The 1975–76 campaign law does not provide for equal protection under the law or for due process, but consigns to a bureaucracy—the Federal Election commission—legislative, executive, and judicial powers. A magisterial proceeding is, in effect, set up—one of the very things that stirred Jefferson and Madison to support the American Revolution. The amendments violate the right of political privacy, something long sought through secret ballot and limitations on public registration along party lines.

Through legitimizing corporate and labor union political action committees, it set in motion a process whereby control over politics must certainly gravitate to these two sources of campaign financing, to the detriment of political parties, other political organizations, and individuals. Candidates of the future are more and more likely to be those supported by corporate funds, as is already being demonstrated in congressional elections, or by union funds, as shown in the nomination of Walter Mondale. The only candidates who may be able to stand against this trend will be individuals of great personal or family wealth, who under the Supreme Court's interpretation of the constitutional guarantee of freedom of speech cannot be limited in their expenditure for political purposes if the money is theirs or their family's.

In effect, the legislation consigns to the government significant control over the process by which the government itself is to be chosen, thus going beyond Alexis de Tocqueville's warning of the danger of tyranny of the majority in a democracy to an even more serious danger, one of the ultimate tyranny—that of the majority over itself.

IS JOHN ADAMS

SAFE FOR DEMOCRACY?

(Washington Star, November 27, 1977)

More than 200 years ago, John Adams, along with his cousin Samuel and others, inspired and led the American Revolution. John Adams believed in self-government. He believed that politics should not be controlled by the British government or any other government.

John Adams warned against the dangers of partisan politics and he especially warned against the dangers of two-party politics. In 1780, commenting on the new Massachusetts Constitution, he wrote: "There is nothing which I dread so much as a division of the republic into two great parties, each arranged under its leader, and converting measures in opposition to each other. This, in my humble apprehension, is to be dreaded as the greatest political evil under our constitution."

In the revolutionary era, John Adams was no favorite of the British government. Had he been captured, he might well have been hanged for his political activities. He escaped such a fate, and eventually became the second president of the United States.

Some 200 years later, another man named John Adams, a New Englander who evidently believed in open politics but was unaware that politics in the United States is not what it was before passage of the Federal Election Campaign Act, encountered the power of the state. Adams in 1976 was moved to run for the Republican nomination for the U.S. House of Representatives from the First District of New Hampshire. The office he sought was then held by a Democrat who was popular with his constituents.

John Adams, sixty-one years old, a U.S. Navy veteran of World War II, suffered from a wartime knee injury and arthritis. His only income was a U.S. Navy disability pension of $173 a month. He filed for the Republican primary and (one assumes because of his good name) won the primary in September of 1976.

Then the Federal Election Commission, the administrative agency of the Federal Election Campaign Act, entered the picture. John Adams came under official watch because he had not filed financial reports required by the law. When he entered the campaign, he apparently did not know that such reports were required.

The FEC sent notices and forms and, eventually, threatening letters; but it received no information about John.

John did, however, respond in one way to the call of the state. After receiving one of the FEC threats, he made a collect call to the FEC office in Washington, saying that he had asked for no money for his campaign, had received none, had spent none, and had called collect because he did not have thirteen cents for a stamp.

This information might have satisfied the commission, since it had no evidence that Adams had collected or spent any money. But the FEC staff had no written reports with which to paper their files.

The case against John Adams was, as the bureaucrats say, "activated." The power of the law and of the courts was turned on John Adams, as it had been turned on his illustrious predecessor of the same name. He became a hunted man and a wanted person—not by the agents of the Crown, but by the agents of the FEC.

The FEC proceeded against Adams in federal court, asking that he be required to file the information demanded, and that he be fined up to $5,000. Adams neither responded to the suit nor appeared in court. The commission continued its case against the "great menace to clean elections," even after he was trounced by the Democratic incumbent in the November election.

Since Adams did not respond to its suit, the FEC filed a default motion in federal court. A hearing was held in Concord, New Hampshire, on January 12, 1977. The commission sent one of its top lawyers to appear before the federal judge. (It is rumored that the judge asked the lawyer if the FEC didn't have better things to do with its time.) Adams did not appear. The judge ordered that he be made to file the required information and that he be fined $100.

The majesty of the federal government, in the person of U.S. marshals, proceeded to search for John Adams. They found him in an old soldiers' home in Massachusetts. He filled out an FEC report, listing a total of $150 in spending—$50 for his primary filing fee and $100 for telephone calls. But he did not pay the fine, possibly because he did not have the money.

The FEC evidently did not think of attaching the culprit's disability pension, or making him sell his war medals, in order to settle the fine.

RESTORE THE
ELECTORAL COLLEGE

(The Federalist Papers, 1987)

The Constitutional Convention, after prolonged debate, and after having considered procedures for choosing a president—election by the national legislature, or by state representatives, or directly by the people—finally approved, by a vote of nine states to two, the principle of electing the president by a body created specifically for that purpose, namely, the Electoral College.

In the first presidential election some electors were appointed by state legislatures. A few other states, including Pennsylvania, Maryland, and Virginia, provided for popular election of the electors.

By 1796, the first election after George Washington's two terms, electors were chosen by the people in six states and by legislatures in ten states. By that time, within eight years of the adoption of the Constitution, partisanship had reached the point that, in every one of the sixteen states then a part of the Union, electors were picked as men pledged to one candidate or the other: John Adams or Thomas Jefferson. The Electoral College as conceived by the Founding Fathers—a body of responsible, trusted persons—was hardly tested.

As partisan politics has become more dominant, the independent role of the Electoral College has been all but forgotten, and electors vote automatically for the party candidate to whom they are committed. Because of the development of partisan politics, and for other reasons, the original conception of how the Electoral College was intended to work has been confused and neglected. A popular opinion has developed that the Electoral College is either a bad idea or one that is unworkable. It is neither. The trouble is that it has not been used as it was intended.

The original conception was that electors would be chosen for one task only, a very important one in the new republic: the selection of a president of the United States. As electors they were to be agents of the people of their states. It was anticipated that the electors would be wise and responsible, that they would be free of involvement with politics and legislative matters because they were not members of Congress or of state legislatures. The Electoral College, as it was called, was designed to deny both Congress and the voters total, direct power over an election. Whereas the Founding Fathers were familiar with political factions—division being the mark of every political society—they hoped and believed that these divisive and power-seeking organizations would have a limited influence in the choice of members of Congress and especially of the president.

The states could, by individual and separate actions, restore the electoral process to what it was intended to be. They are as unlikely to do so as they were to extend the vote to women or to persons between the ages of eighteen and twenty-one before constitutional amendments accomplishing those purposes were adopted. Maine is the only state that has moved, even modestly, to conform to the constitutional intent.

The Maine system—by which one electoral vote goes to the winner of the popular vote in each congressional district and two electoral votes go to the winner of the statewide popular vote—is clearly better than the winner-take-all rule applied in the other forty-nine states. Better than the Maine district system would be one dividing the states into presidential electoral districts, each smaller than a congressional district, which now includes about 450,000 persons.

If each presidential elector represented, say, a district of 100,000 persons, a candidate for the Electoral College could campaign effectively without spending great sums of money. One person with a few volunteers could, in the course of a presidential campaign, reach all voters in his 100,000-person constituency. If the country were divided into some 2,000 such districts, 2,000 presidential electors would be chosen. Obviously, if a majority of those chosen were Democrats, a Democratic president would be chosen; if a majority were Republicans, a Republican would be president. If neither party had a majority, the third- or fourth-party electors would hold the balance of power and their votes would have to be solicited by other parties.

This procedure is no different from the one followed within U.S. political parties at their conventions (or on the way to conventions). In Great Britain it is used in choosing the prime minister, under the parliamentary system.

A president chosen through this process would clearly be a constitutional president, and he or she would be chosen by electors who represented a majority—if not of the voters, almost certainly of the citizens.

We should follow the advice of John Holcombe, who, in the early years of this century, argued that "in no reactionary spirit, therefore, but with views thoroughly progressive," we should "return for relief to the wisdom of the fathers by making effective their admirable device—the Electoral College."

In so speaking, he sustained the judgment of James Madison, not only as expressed in the Constitution, but as late as 1823, when he wrote, "One advantage of electors is that, although generally the mere mouths of their constituents, they may be intentionally left sometimes, to their own judgment, guided by further information that may be acquired for them; and finally, what is of material importance, they will be able, when ascertaining which may not be till a late hour, that the first choice of their constituents is utterly hopeless, to substitute in the Electoral College the name known to be their second choice."

The need for purifying and perfecting the process of the selection of the president is most important at this time, because of the complexity and weight of the demands of the presidential office and because voter knowledge of the qualifications of the presidential candidates is obscured or distorted with the intrusion of media hype. Yet it is better to improve the representative process, as conceived by Madison, than to propose that it should be done away with because the representative process has not worked in the Electoral College. The problem is not the defects in the conception of that constitutional institution but, rather, the intrusion of partisanship and the intervention of political parties and conventions between the people and the Electoral College.

THE RULES
DETERMINE THE WINNER

(1988)

In 1984 Jesse Jackson and Gary Hart, among others, discovered that
the fix was on—that the Democratic party had changed its rules
again, and that rules rather than issues or personalities would once
more, as had been the case in 1968, 1972, 1976, and 1980, determine who would be the party's nominee. In addition to the rule
changes, there is the significant fact that in each convention since
that of 1968, the person who was nominated played a significant
part in revising the rules for the convention and the nominating
process through which he was chosen as the party's presidential
candidate.

The quadrennial changing of the rules began following the convention of 1968. The convention of that year, in which Hubert Humphrey was chosen as the party's nominee, was conducted according to the traditional rules and practices of the Democratic party. Delegate selection and voting practices were left largely to the states. Winner-take-all primary results were accepted. Delegations from nonprimary states were permitted to vote according to the unit rule—that is, to vote the whole state delegation according to the determination of the majority. In the 1968 convention there were two exceptions to the practice of allowing state rules to apply. The Mississippi delegation was rejected on the grounds of underrepresentation of blacks (a precedent for George McGovern's exploitation of the quota principle in the 1972 convention); and the Lester Maddox-Georgia delegation was challenged on grounds of racial discrimination, party loyalty, and nonrepresentation of differing ideological views. The credentials committee of the convention, applying one of the worst guides drawn from Solomon's most serious failure in the halls of justice, split the vote between the Maddox group and the challengers. The breakup of the Georgia delegation on the basis of ideological differences was an innovation in Democratic political action. Georgia was the only state whose delegation was revised on these grounds. When a similar challenge was raised against other delegations, the Humphrey supporters objected, saying that they would not do a democratic thing by undemocratic means.

Under pressure because of inequitable and discriminatory practices, the 1968 convention adopted a resolution specifying that the delegates to the next convention would have to be chosen more democratically. That resolution became the basis for the McGovern Reform Commission, which determined the rules for the 1972 convention. Although I had had some interest in the 1968 convention, the party did not place me on the commission. I agreed with Senator Humphrey, who said, when asked about his part in the proceedings of the commission, that he had had no representative in "the skunk works." Humphrey lost the nomination in 1972.

The rules that were adopted eliminated the unit rule in delegate selection in nonprimary states and prohibited secret slatemaking. They laid down some general principles that were later identified and applied as requiring "quotas" of nearly every identifiable minority in the Democratic party.

The 1972 rules proved to be just what were needed to ensure the nomination of George McGovern. Whereas the unit rule was outlawed, thus assuring McGovern his share of delegates from nonprimary states, the winner-take-all and other primary laws were not challenged. Consequently, with 44 percent of the vote in the California primary, George received 100 percent of the California delegates. By applying the same rule, he also received all of the delegates from Oregon, Rhode Island, and South Dakota.

Application of the new rules against secret slatemaking and those requiring proper and proportional representation of minorities and of women (not a minority) led to the rejection of Mayor Richard Daley's Chicago delegation of fifty-nine persons. They were replaced by a largely pro-McGovern delegation made up of blacks, Hispanics, and women, in proportion to their presence in the Chicago population.

Following the 1972 convention, the Democrats again moved to change the rules. In this effort, the principal target was the obviously discriminatory treatment of states with primaries in which the unit rule was allowed to apply and the treatment of states that did not have primaries and acted through nominating conventions. The chairman of the post-1972 Commission on Rules was Leonard Woodcock, president of the United Auto Workers. One of the active commission members was Jimmy Carter.

Woodcock was subsequently the first major labor leader to endorse Carter for president. The rules adopted for the 1976 convention served the Carter presidential effort admirably. The new rules eliminated the winner-take-all primary. This meant that in states that held primaries, Carter was to receive his share of the delegates according to his popular vote. Carter did marginally well in states that held primaries, so he got a good number of delegates that, under winner-take-all rules, he would not have received. In nonprimary states, especially in the South, he did not need a unit rule, since he received nearly all of the delegates. It is quite probable that without the rule changes adopted in advance of the 1976 nominating process, Carter would not have been nominated, and Mo Udall, Frank Church, or possibly Senator Humphrey might have been chosen. Certainly Carter would have had great difficulty in securing the nomination.

The Carter-controlled Democratic National Committee quite prudently foresaw that President Carter might have difficulty in getting the party nomination in 1980 if the 1976 rules were left in force. The rules were changed in 1978 in the name of reform. Liberals, who are in the habit of supporting anything labeled "reform," supported the change. In order to be a successful peanut processor, as Carter had been, one has to be able to think "small."

Although the new rules did not quite ensure Carter's renomination, they gave him a clear advantage over challengers, especially if there were a number of challengers. Shortly before Senator Edward Kennedy announced his candidacy, a Carter campaign spokesperson observed that because of the new rules and the new provisons of federal law bearing principally on the limitations of personal campaign expenditures and other legal campaign restrictions, Edward Kennedy's campaign would be much more difficult than those of his brothers John and Robert.

The key to the new rules, however, was something called "the threshold"—a percentage below which a candidate would receive no delegate votes. The exact threshold level was never quite clearly established. The original formula held that the threshold was to be determined by dividing 100 percent by the number of delegates in the voting district, or in the state if the state was considered as a whole voting district. In a five-delegate district, for example, the threshold would be 100 divided by five, or 20. Thus, any candidate getting under 20 percent would receive no delegate votes. Thus—as it was explained at the time—if in a four-candidate race the popular vote was 46-29-21-4, the winner would get two delegates and each of the next two candidates would get one. The fourth candidate would get none. The fifth delegate, however, would not go to the person who had received the highest percentage of votes, but rather to the candidate who had the highest percentage of votes after subtracting the threshold figure from the percentage vote of the top candidate. Thus, by subtracting 20 percent from the 46 percent received by the leading candidate, that candidate would be left with only 26 percent, three points less than the 29 percent of the second-place finisher, who would then be entitled to the leftover vote.

The application of the threshold rule had varying effects, depending on the sizes of states and electoral districts, and other peculiarities of state laws and election practices. In Massachusetts, its application assured at least one delegate to a candidate who received only 2.381 percent of the vote. In Idaho, 80 percent of the delegates would be distributed among candidates who achieved or surpassed a threshold that was determined at 5 percent. In North Carolina, delegates were to be allotted proportionately to candidates who received at least 10 percent of the popular vote. In Oregon, delegates were to be allocated proportionately to the nearest whole number. The net effect of the changes in the rules was to give to the incumbent, Jimmy Carter—who was certain to finish first in many states and not lower than second in most other states—an advantage over a field of challengers, some of whom might do well in a few states or districts and badly in many others.

Calculators—rather than programs or noisemakers and paper hats—were most important along the way to the nomination of Jimmy Carter in 1980.

Not content to go along with the restrictive, incumbent-ensuring rules of the 1980 campaign, Democratic party leaders, officeholders, and officials of the labor movement have moved to make the rules for convention delegate selection even more restrictive. Certainly former vice president Walter Mondale was involved in the rule changes. There have been assertions that Senator Kennedy or his agents were also involved. These assertions have been challenged by Kennedy spokesmen; Mondale has not denied his involvement.

The advantages to the "chosen one" follow from three rule changes. One is called "front-loading," the compression of primaries and caucuses into a short time period. According to the party rules for 1984, almost half of the delegates to the Democratic convention will be chosen within a thirty-six-day period following the Iowa caucus on February 27, 1984. Under the old rules, candidates had time to build support: in 1968, for example, the time period was late February or early March (the New Hampshire primary) until early June (the New York primary).

A second advantage given to the front-runner, the incumbent, or the core-control group in a party (in the case of the Democratic party, including the labor movement as an important if not the most important component) is the rule change allowing the application of the unit rule not statewide but by congressional districts, coupled with an approximate 20-percent threshold requirement for eligibility for delegate allocation within any state.

The third advantage given to central control is the allocation of 550 delegate places to elected officials, members of Congress, and local officials—about 14 percent of all delegates.

In working out these changes Walter Mondale, the prospective nominee, has played a prominent part in arranging procedures to, if not ensure, at least make more certain his nomination.

The whole procedure conforms to at least one of Parkinson's laws: Institutions or persons in trouble try to ensure survival, through procedural and legal support. The reality is that with the rules for the Democratic nomination process for 1984, the party has not regressed to the undemocratic procedures of 1968, but has adopted rules that are more restrictive, more undemocratic, more clearly in violation of the principle of "one person, one vote," and more centrally controlling than were the rules of 1968.

It is not a case of a majority overriding even consideration of minorities or minority interests in the party, but rather a case of adopting and applying rules through which a minority of the party can override and control the majority. The rules go beyond the "tyranny of the majority," which de Tocqueville saw as the inherent danger of democracy, to the further, possibly ultimate, corruption or perversion of the democratic process. In this scenario, the stage is set through rules or laws, for the tyranny of a minority, established by the majority, over the majority itself.

WHAT TO DO ABOUT
THE PRESIDENTIAL SELECTION
AND ELECTION PROCESS

(1983)

Positive suggestions for improving the election process are difficult to propose, since basically what is called for is responsible decision on the part of the electorate, sustained and assisted by a creditable press.

Procedural changes are possible, however, clearing the way to responsible decision making. There are at least four such changes that would be useful and easily achieved. They could be effected without seriously interfering with freedom of speech or assembly—the two basic constitutional rights that bear on political choice.

• The office of vice president should be abolished. Provisions for replacing a president in an orderly, rational, and prompt way could be applied, similar to the procedures outlined in the constitutional amendment on presidential disability. They worked well enough when Gerald Ford was chosen to replace Spiro Agnew, following Agnew's resignation. There are at least three good reasons for abolishing the office. First, having a vice president on the ticket clutters the election campaign, offering the voters an apparent choice when in fact only the presidential candidate will— while he lives—be in a position to direct and significantly affect policy. And, in principle, a ticket made up of two unbalanced persons might well appear to constitute a balanced ticket.

Second, the existence of the office of the vice president puts persons in line for the presidency who would not necessarily be the best choice to run for that office. Recent examples include Richard Nixon, who probably could not have made it to the candidacy had he not been vice president under Eisenhower. Lyndon Johnson had had no success in his efforts to win the presidential nomination prior to his becoming vice president. This applies certainly to Spiro Agnew, who had no national political reputation and no known qualifications for the presidency when chosen (one must assume for purely political reasons) to be Richard Nixon's running mate.

Third, the office can waste the abilities of a good politician for four or eight years, years during which he or she could serve more effectively in some other office. Examples include Lyndon Johnson and Hubert Humphrey, whose talents went unused when he served as vice president. Holding the office may also seriously impair the officeholder's chances of being elected president, even though it may help to get him nominated. It is commonly held that both Humphrey and Walter Mondale were hurt as presidential candidates by their vice-presidential services.

• Another positive suggestion toward improving election processes is that the Federal Election Campaign Act amendments of 1975–76 should be repealed, opening the political process as it was open before that legislation was passed. A procedure that brought to the country such presidents as Franklin Roosevelt, Harry Truman, Dwight Eisenhower, and John Kennedy, in contrast with President Carter and President Reagan, cannot be judged to have been all bad.

The American Revolution could not have been waged if laws in any way comparable to current federal election laws had been in effect, nor could the antiwar campaign of 1968 been organized or carried on effectively.

• Televised political advertisements should be abolished. Or, if that is not possible, severely regulated so as to minimize the conditioning effects of current ads. The country now forbids televised advertising of liquor and cigarettes, presumably protecting U.S. citizens from physical corruption. Similar bans should be applied to the other end of the spectrum of human needs and wants—namely, politics and religion. Television could continue to carry ads for deodorants, detergents, pain relief, and automobiles.

The equal-time and fairness doctrines should be rigorously applied to televised reporting of political campaigns, even though the presentation of such news might be severely limited as a result. The spoken word (primarily radio) and the written word remain the best means of political reportage. For it was in the period approximately from 1930 to 1960—after the advent of radio and before the coming of television—that the best communication of political ideas took place.

• Finally, televised debates should be eliminated, unless used as a device to attract the attention of voters during primaries—a compromise justification. But they are best wholly banned in the showdown campaign between major candidates. Presidents, unlike Senators, do not have to be great debaters. Once elected, they will not be debating anyone. Most candidates admit that the persons who most influence them are their spouses (and second, their vice presidents). If a debate is to have significant bearing on the presidency, perhaps it should be held between the presidential candidate and his or her spouse; or between the presidential and vice-presidential candidates of the same party.

If interparty debates are to be held, they could be presented in the format of tag-team wrestling, with any one of the three team members being sent to argue with any one of the members of the other three-person team.

With the course cleared by these changes, there would be time to look to the positive and substantive basis upon which presidents should be chosen—to procedures for primaries and caucuses, and to state laws governing the selection and election of presidential candidates.

INALIENABLE DUTIES

(Address, Yale Political Union, September 17, 1987)

The Declaration of Independence makes clear reference to the "inalienable rights" of all men. Among those rights, it declares, are three of particular political significance: life, liberty, and the pursuit of happiness.

The *duties of citizenship*, essential to securing and sustaining these inalienable rights, however, are not mentioned directly in the Declaration of Independence or in the Constitution, but their necessity and reality were implicit in the very conception of self-government. Today, I would like to discuss these fundamental responsibilities, or inalienable duties, which are: (1) to defend the country and its government; (2) to pay taxes to meet the costs of government; and (3) to participate in the political actions that are essential to self-government.

There was no searching inquiry into defense and into war-making at the Constitutional Convention, but providing for the common defense is listed as one of the fundamental purposes of the new government. The inclusion of the right to bear arms in the Bill of Rights was related to the need for national as well as personal self-defense. It was not included to protect the rights of squirrel hunters.

As early as 1785, well before he became president, Thomas Jefferson recognized the need for military and naval operations when he wrote to John Jay from Paris: "Our people are decided in the opinion that it is necessary for us to take a share in the occupation of the ocean, and their established habits induce them to require that the sea be kept open to them. . . . Therefore," he continued, "we should in every instance (even at the cost of war) preserve an equality of right to them in the transportation of commodities, in the right of fishing and in the other uses of the sea."

As president, Jefferson took action against the Barbary pirates. His later experience with the embargo of American goods and his observation of the War of 1812 moved him to an even stronger military position. Although he did not go so far as to support Alexander Hamilton, who wanted a standing army, he came to believe that serious thought must be given to the maintenance of a military establishment, which he thought should be, in a democracy, based upon universal military service or liability for such service. He wrote to James Monroe in 1813: "It is more a subject of joy that we have so few of the desperate characters which compose modern regular armies. But it proves more forcibly the necessity of obliging every citizen to be a soldier. This was the case with Greeks and Romans and must be that of every free state. . . . We must train and classify the whole of our male citizens and make military instruction a regular part of collegiate education. We cannot be safe till this is done." The safety he was concerned about related to two threats: outside military action against the United States and the internal danger of a mercenary, nonrepresentative army.

No policy of military conscription was established. In 1831 Alexis de Tocqueville noted that the United States Army consisted of 6,000 soldiers and that the United States Navy had only a few ships. Internal disturbances were left largely to state militia. In 1860, thirty years after de Tocqueville's visit, the regular army of the United States had 16,257 men. The Navy had forty vessels in commission, and these were scattered over the oceans and seas of the world.

A stronger national military organization, at that time, might have prevented the Civil War. In April of 1861, President Abraham Lincoln called for 75,000 volunteers who were to serve for three months. In May, he called for forty volunteer regiments, each averaging 1,050 men, and for an additional 40,000 three-year enlistments, in the regular army and navy. The recruiting, organizing, and equipping of volunteer regiments was left to the states. By the winter of 1862–63, it was evident that the volunteer approach was not adequate to meet Union needs, and a conscription act was passed in March of 1863. The law was, in the judgment of historian Samuel Eliot Morison, ". . . a most imperfect law, a travesty of conscription." Morison had not seen the draft law administered during the Vietnam War by the Johnson and the Nixon administrations.

At the outbreak of World War I, the United States had a navy of limited readiness and an army numbering about 200,000 officers and men, which included 67,000 National Guardsmen. A draft registration act was passed on June 3, 1916, and another in 1918. Overall, 24.2 million men registered, of whom 2.2 million were actually inducted.

In 1940 a draft act again was passed as preliminary to full involvement in World War II. In 1951 that act was extended for twenty years, to meet the needs of the Korean War, and then allowed to expire during the Nixon administration. This era, 1941–1971, was the only prolonged period during which the United States did, in effect, have a universal military service program. Not all males of eligible age were called up, but all were formally subject to the draft. Before the act was allowed to die, it had been—first in the Johnson administration and then in the Nixon administration— thoroughly corrupted through the granting of many exemptions, especially to students of almost every kind, in an effort to insulate the war from Americans who might be most likely to criticize it if they or their children were forced into it. Since the Johnson administration believed the war would end quickly, it did not anticipate having to answer for its exemptions. But the war did not end quickly, and the Nixon administration followed a similar policy of exemptions, with the addition of a new device under which a potential draftee could decide within a range of three or four years when he or she would be subject to the draft.

As the war was winding down in the early seventies, the draft law expired. No attempt to extend it was made in the Nixon administration, and the drive to establish a large "volunteer" army was initiated. This proposal was supported by militarists, based on their belief that only militarily minded persons, either by their nature or by their commitment, would make up the military forces. Consequently, the United States, they believed, would have a ready and uncritical military force.

Antimilitarists in general, and anti-Vietnam War activists in particular, accepted and supported the volunteer proposal because they thought that their consciences, and the consciences of others in the future, would be eased if they would not have to perform military services.

The volunteer army idea has not worked well. The Department of Defense has not been able to attract enough capable and qualified persons to the armed services. Our armed forces are far from a cross section of the U.S. population; our military is unrepresentative of the nation. Standards of admission have been lowered; financial and other benefits have been increased; cash bonuses for enlisting have been offered.

The "volunteer army" has been a designation for what is essentially a "mercenary army." De Tocqueville and others have warned that such a military is the most dangerous and undesirable type for a democratic state. This is especially true when a major function of our military is to act as an army of occupation, or as a presence—as ours is in Europe, in Japan, in Korea, and in other parts of the world.

The second inalienable duty recognized in the Constitution is the responsibility of citizens to pay taxes. The revolutionary slogan "Taxation without representation is tyranny" is credited to James Otis. Otis did not say, "Taxation with representation is tyranny" or that taxation in itself is tyrannical, or that in the ideal state, citizens would pay few or no taxes. The Sixteenth Amendment, the so-called income-tax amendment, was the last formal acknowledgment on the part of the people of the United States of their willingness to pay taxes ". . . to pay the debts and provide for the common defense and general welfare of the United States," as stated in Article 1 of the Constitution.

Recent U.S. presidents and presidential candidates seem to have a different attitude toward taxes. Candidate Jimmy Carter said that the federal tax code ". . . was a disgrace to the human race"—a questionable remark, since most of that code had been written by Democratic Congresses. As candidate and as president, Ronald Reagan has generally opposed taxes, while annual federal deficits run to hundreds of billions and the federal debt is well into its third trillion. His slogan, in the Otis manner, might well be a declaration in favor of "representation without taxation," which in its consequences as a policy may well be as tyrannous as the colonial "taxation without representation."

Opposition to paying taxes, or to imposing them on citizens, is not limited to presidential and other candidates and officeholders. Antitaxation programs are sustained by individuals, by their representatives, by lobbyists, by foundations, by corporations. The drive to eliminate taxpaying, to avoid payment or to be exempted, is manifest at all levels of taxpaying and directed against nearly every form of taxation, but it is especially evident at the higher and lower levels of income-tax liabilities. The reasons given for exempting citizens from tax obligations are multiple. Such words as *fairness* and *equity* are invoked regularly. Concern is voiced for the poor and for persons in low-income brackets. Efficiency in the administration of tax law, simplification of the code, stimulation of business, encouragement of capital formation and savings—all are among the reasons or justifications offered. Lobbyists and various representatives—individual and institutional—are quick to take credit for eliminating high-level income-tax obligations, or for reducing them. Politicians generally—Republicans and Democrats, liberals and conservatives—claim credit for reduction or elimination of tax obligations at the lower end of the income scale.

According to studies by the Brookings Institution, there are about 131 million potential tax units. Of these, it is projected that about 108 million will file tax returns. Some 20 million persons, or tax units, will not file because of income insufficiency. Of the 108 million filers, about 17 million will pay no taxes this year; 23.7 million will pay no taxes when the most recent tax reform bill is operative.

When the 1986 tax bill was under consideration, Democrats and Republicans boasted of the number of persons who would be excluded from paying the basic federal taxes.

According to the Brookings estimates, in 1988 approximately 50 million out of 130 million potential taxpayers (or approximately 38 percent) will pay no taxes (that is, basic income and capital gains taxes to the federal government), thus creating two classes of citizens—one paying basic taxes and the other exempted for varying reasons from fulfilling even in a minimal way this obligation of citizenship. John Wesley is supposed to have said that even in the church some small financial contribution should be expected, if not extracted. Certainly the same would seem to be true of support for civil government, even though the rate is very low. Alexis de Tocqueville reported that in 1831, during his visit to the United States, fifteen out of the existing twenty-four states required property ownership, military service, or tax payment as a prerequisite to voting.

Thus far I have described what has happened to two of the inalienable duties of citizenship—military service and paying taxes. The third is "participation in political action and decisions."

Jefferson warned that if the people became indifferent to politics and to government, the magistrates (an early version of the bureaucrats) would take over. Although there were serious restrictions on suffrage in the early decades of our national existence, those who had the right to vote evidently took their responsibility seriously.

Alexis de Tocqueville was greatly impressed by what he saw or was told, for he wrote in *Democracy in America* in 1831: "To take a hand in the government of society and to talk about it is his [the American citizen's] most important business and, so to say, the only pleasure he knows." He continued: "If an American should be reduced to occupying himself with his own affairs, at that moment, half his existence would be snatched from him; he would feel it as a vast void in his life and would become incredibly unhappy."

In the 1986 off-year election, the percentage of eligible American voters who cast their ballots dropped to its lowest level since the World War II year of 1942, and it was the third-lowest turnout in American history. Voting in states outside the thirteen southern states was the lowest in American history, according to the findings and report of the Committee for the Study of the American Electorate. In the 1986 national election, an estimated 66.25 million voters cast their ballots, leaving 112 million who failed to vote, out of approximately 178 million potentially eligible voters. The percentage of eligible voters who went to the polls was approximately 37 percent.

Undoubtedly many voters were kept from participating by unreasonable registration and residence requirements; by state laws giving special preference to the Republican and the Democratic parties; by laws making it difficult for third- or independent-party candidates to get on the ballot; by machine voting, which makes write-in campaigns practically impossible; and by restrictive party rules.

Some analysts attribute declining and low voter turnouts, in part, to such factors as the high mobility of the American population, disenchantment with the conduct of politics, and the deadening and distracting effect of television generally and especially in politics.

After every campaign, politicians and press deplore low voter turnout. Thus, as each campaign approaches or begins, they encourage political participation and support "get out the vote" drives. In anticipation of the 1988 elections, "get out the vote" organizations proliferated. There is a Southwest Voters' Registration organization in Arizona, with a special goal of getting the Navajo nation ready for political action. "Project Vote" has been started in at least nine states. Its purpose is to register one million new voters in low-income and minority communities. Both the NAACP and the League of Women Voters have announced registration drives. Many more organizations will follow.

At the same time that the drives for voting participation go on, legislative and political actions of various kinds discourage citizens from full participation in politics. Whereas the poll tax has been outlawed as an impediment to participation in political action, in its place, public records and reports of financial contributions, even minimal ones, are now required in many states. Complicated reports are required in many jurisdictions. But more significant than all of these local and state controls and interferences with basic and fundamental participation in politics is the Federal Election Campaign Act as amended in 1975–76. The law not only sets severe limitations on financial contributions to campaigns, but also provides for government financing of political action with operating control centered in the Federal Election Commission. Under this law, citizens' participation in, and possibly influence on, politics is restricted, and government and corporate influence and control are increased. In essence, the law puts the government in a position to significantly and substantively influence the process by which the government itself is established. This procedure, which we now have accepted as one supposed to ensure good and democratic government, was essentially like what existed when Hitler was elected in Germany. Not only does the 1975–76 law limit and discourage individual contributions and commitment, but it encourages and strengthens intermediary organizations (the political action committees) to further depersonalize politics and come between citizen and politics and government. Whereas individual contributions to a campaign are effectively limited, the same amount contributed through a PAC is multiplied in power, but only at the sacrifice of the independent judgment of the contributing citizen.

Another institutional force preventing greater personal participation in politics is that of reform organizations themselves, most notably Common Cause. That organization, in its appeals for money, advises prospective contributors that they need not perform volunteer activities, or do anything except send money. "Trust Common Cause," the appeals, in effect, say, "to represent you politically along the way."

And so we find ourselves in 1988, the bicentennial of the adoption of the Constitution, with the three inalienable duties of citizenship and our democracy seriously compromised. First, we have compromised military service with the initiation of the volunteer (mercenary) army, in the Nixon administration; second, we have exempted many of our citizens from responsibility for paying taxes, an achievement noted and claimed as a credit by Democrats and Republicans, especially in the latest tax bill; and third, we have transferred fundamental political responsibility for financing and for political action from citizens and committees to the government and governmentally approved political units, the PACs. (This last was accomplished in the administration of Gerald Ford, who said when he signed the bill that he thought it unconstitutional but would leave the decision to the courts.)

The whole complex has given good service to the candidacies of Ronald Reagan, who has been the most persistent and most outspoken opponent of government intervention and of government subsidies, and at the same time the most subsidized politician in the history of the world.

Part II

OF SUBSTANCE—SENSE AND

NONSENSE

MUSICAL WARS

(*New Republic*, JANUARY 20, 1982)

It was bound to be found: the money for military bands and other musical units in the Defense Department budget recommendations. And what was discovered was not only that the Reagan administration plans no cuts in these appropriations, but that it proposes, contrary to its general reductionist bent, to increase the musically martial money for the next fiscal year to $89.7 million.

This fortissimo spending is under attack from three separate and distinct enemies. The first group is the pure budget cutters, of which a subspecies holds that if the budget is cut anywhere it should be cut everywhere, without distinction or prejudice. They hold that if the fat is to be omitted from the defense budget, then military music should be muted too. If the nation can get along with fewer food stamps and not so many MX missiles, they ask, why can't it get along with fewer tubas?

The second line of attack is from members of Congress who have risen above financial considerations where the defense budget is concerned but question the impact of music upon national security. Some of these—the militarists who fear that the West is losing the will to resist—have heard that "music hath charms to soothe the savage breast." They worry that too much, especially of the gentler or the more syncopated kind, being played by some military ensembles may dull the military spirit.

The third front on which the military musicians are besieged is manned and womanned by lovers of better music and the higher culture. They do not argue directly against the military bands appropriations, but rather make the relative argument that these outlays should not be increased if, as recommended by the Reagan administration, the appropriation for support of the civilian arts is to be cut by 50 percent to a mere $77 million—approximately $13 million less than that being proposed for the uniformed instrumentalists. Senator Edward Kennedy, in a letter asking for contributions to his Fund for a Democratic Majority, makes a special point of calling attention to these budget items. He writes: "The new military budget, for example, contains more money—$89.9 million—for military bands than the entire budget proposed for the National Endowment for the Arts." And Representative Fred Richmond of New York, addressing the same point, said, "There are three full (military) bands in the Washington area, and each of them has a larger budget than the National Symphony Orchestra." He added, "I don't think it's fair."

Whether the appropriations are unfair is open to challenge. Obviously they are not equitable in comparison with those proposed for the National Endowment for the Arts. But the case against the military music appropriations cannot be made successfully on grounds of equity and fairness. There are deeper and more complex forces operating here.

Maintaining separate musical units has always been a mark of pride and of practicality among the separate services. The popularity of the Marine Band was a formidable obstacle when the Pentagon, during the early 1960s, attempted to liquidate the Marine Corps. Secretary of Defense Robert McNamara, in his efforts to unify the armed forces, never got to the point of trying to unify the bands. He was routed far earlier. But it was suspected that he did have long-range contingency plans for an eventual try at melding the musical groups of the various branches of the armed forces. These plans were never activated, possibly because of the failure of his effort to provide one fighter airplane, originally known as the TFX, which, it was projected, would satisfy the needs of all branches of the armed services. The same fate befell a proposal to have one religion for the whole military establishment—a kind of GI religion that would be taken up when a person enlisted and left behind when he or she was discharged.

It is not only separation among the forces that is at issue here; it is also the competition among them. The growth of music appropriations for the armed forces reflects, in addition to the general growth in military spending, the rivalry among the services for possession and control of weapons and weapons systems.

In arms competition, each branch of our armed forces seeks to be fully prepared to carry out the three kinds of possible military action, defined by the Pentagon as conventional war, unconventional (nuclear) war, and irregular, or "guerrilla," war. In the realm of music, they seek to be similarly flexible.

The bedrock of musical preparedness is, of course, the conventional military band. In this category are the basic marching bands of the Army, the Navy, the Air Force, and the Marine Corps. Like the Pentagon itself, these bands tend to be heavy on the brass. The Army has fifty basic bands. The Navy has seventeen, some of which are equipped with life jackets. The Marine Corps has ten. And the

Air Force has twenty, which can be roughly divided into categories comparable to bombing wings, fighter wings, and missile emplacements.

In addition to the marching bands, the separate services each have a variety of "unconventional" and "irregular" musical groups. On the choral front, the Army is clearly ahead, since it can call upon the massed vocal power of the U.S. Army Chorus. The Navy has the "Sea Chanters" and the Air Force has the "Singing Sergeants." In the jazz theatre of operations, the Army deploys a unit known as the "Army Blues"; the Navy's able-bodied jazzmen are called "The Commodores"; and the Air Force, at a moment's notice, can scramble a jazz combo called "Airmen of Note."

The Army, in its diversified musical arsenal, has a chamber orchestra, a brass quartet, a string quartet, a unit called the "Herald Trumpets" (specializing in fanfares), and a fife-and-drum corps.

The Navy counters with an elite instrumental combo, "Cross Current." The Navy also has a country bluegrass group, as well as "Port Authority," which plays rock and roll. The latter groups, the Navy says, are used principally for recruiting. The Navy has no string groups, leaving a dangerous window of vulnerability in its Mantovani-class strike force. The Air Force, however, partially closes the gap with "The Strolling Strings." The Air Force also has a rapid-deployment rock band called "Mach I." It once had a unit of Scottish pipes, since discontinued in favor of all-weather musical technology.

The Marine Corps makes a point of not breaking its musicians into specialized units. This is consistent with the Corps's tradition of going anywhere and of doing anything it is called upon to do. Its spokesperson says that members of the Marine Band can be selected, on request, to perform any kind of musical mission from Bach to rock; from band and orchestra, combo and ensemble, to solo work on instruments such as guitar and harp; from the Halls of Montezuma to (as seems increasingly likely) the shores of Tripoli.

I discovered the seriousness of the musical competition among the armed services some fifteen years ago, when, as a Senator, I was approached by a spokesman for the Navy about a nomination for appointment to the United States Naval Academy at Annapolis. I anticipated that he might have a football player in mind, or possibly a hockey player, since Minnesota was the best domestic source of college hockey players when the colleges and academies first began to show an interest in that sport. But it was not an athlete the Navy was seeking. It was a young man who could play the French horn. They had recruited well. I nominated their choice for the academy. In the end, he decided not to go, but he did eventually serve with distinction in the Minneapolis Symphony Orchestra.

The emphasis on musical units in the military demonstrates the validity of an observation made by de Tocqueville in *Democracy in America*—namely, that a large military establishment in a democracy, during a long period of relative peace, begins to take on the character of a separate civil society, developing within itself institutions comparable to those that exist in the civilian realm. Thus, our military has its own retirement program, its own educational system, its own newspapers, its own medical service, and its own retail distribution system, the PX—second only, according to a recent study, to Sears, Roebuck in its volume of distribution. And of course it has its own musical units, paralleling, imitating, and in some cases improving upon the nonmilitary society's music. Some of these military bands are really quite good. So if it is true that military intelligence is to intelligence as military music is to music, there may yet be hope for the efficacy of American espionage.

HAMILTON, TOO OPTIMISTIC

(Rushville Republican, AUGUST 7, 1979)

Among the Founding Fathers and the authors of the *Federalist Papers*, Alexander Hamilton was never looked upon as an optimist. He was not seen as being overtrustful of human nature, as might be said of Thomas Jefferson, possibly of James Madison, and (with reservations) of John Adams.

But, set against some of the current assertions of federal government control over highly personal matters, and over matters that could well be left to local decisions without in any way endangering the stability of the commonwealth, Hamilton was far and away too optimistic.

For example, the Federal Trade Commission is moving into regulation of funerals. The FTC's claim to jurisdiction, surprisingly, has gone unchallenged by the Department of Health, Education, and Welfare (now Health and Human Services, HHS) and also by the Department of Transportation.

Joseph Califano, as secretary of HEW, challenged Robert Bergland, secretary of agriculture, on the matter of which department should have jurisdiction over the killing and processing of chickens. Califano apparently lost that battle even before he lost HEW.

The Department of Agriculture proposed a regulation that all schools receiving federal aid for school lunch programs must forbid all vending of certain "junk foods" (chewing gum, soda pop, some candies) until after lunch.

Why such sales should be allowed after lunch, the government agency does not explain. Nor does it explain why students who buy junk food before lunchtime (and therefore, it is believed, skip their school lunches) will not skip lunch in any case and wait for the vending machines to become operative.

All of these assertions of authority prove how wrong Hamilton was when, in *Federalist Paper* no. 17, he undertook to answer the charge that under the proposed Constitution the federal government might become so strong that it would absorb "those residuary authorities, which it might be judged proper to leave with the states for local purposes."

Not anticipating the FTC commissioners or Califano, Hamilton wrote: "Allowing the utmost latitude to the love of power which any reasonable man can require, I confess I am at a loss to discover what temptation the persons entrusted with the administration of the general government could ever feel to divest the states of the authorities of that description."

He then listed some of the things he thought would never be "desirable cares of a general jurisdiction." Among them he included domestic police, supervision of agriculture, and local needs in general.

He concluded: "It is therefore improbable that there should exist a disposition in the federal councils to usurp the powers with which they are connected; because the attempt to exercise those powers would be as troublesome as it would be nugatory; and the possession of them, for that reason, would contribute nothing to the dignity, to the importance, or to the splendor of the national government."

Hamilton did not, of course, anticipate the shared funding of local activities by the federal government and state and local governments. He could not have been expected to foresee that it is the nature of a bureaucracy—once given open-ended responsibility for consumer protection—to expand the definition of who or what a consumer is, dead or alive.

It is the nature of a bureaucracy to pursue that responsibility through the regulation of eating habits, even until and slightly beyond the point at which "death us do part"—with a minor struggle over who supervises the killing of chickens along the way.

NUCLEAR CODES:

DON'T LEAVE HOME

WITHOUT THEM

(*Culpeper News*, JANUARY 28, 1982)

A common and often-repeated assertion of President Reagan is that "Anything, or nearly anything, that the government [otherwise known as the public sector] can do, the private sector can do better."

The administration has not gone so far as to include national defense as a transferable responsibility. It does not advocate selling the ships of the Navy to privateers nor contracting air and land defenses to corporations or to a mercenary army. But it is very positive about the greater competence of private enterprise in the economic order and about placing the responsibility for art and cul-

71

ture on persons and organizations other than the government. Bridges and roads, many of which in the early history of the country were privately owned, are secure in the public sector, protected by state highway departments and by the road builders of America.

I have long thought that the administration had oversimplified the case and that some of the responsibilities and powers that it wished to discard or transfer were better kept in the federal government, whereas some that it wished to keep might be better yielded. Responsibility for income-tax collection might be taken from the Internal Revenue Service and offered to tax farmers, the publicans of the Scriptures, to a modern version of the bounty hunter, or to H. and R. Block, the most trusted men in America (after Walter Cronkite). Block and company's advice has been found in some test cases to be more consistent and accurate than that given by Internal Revenue agents. Block could combine two functions—giving advice and immediately collecting the taxes, thus avoiding delay, duplication, and waste.

A report in the *Washington Post* of December 13, 1981, has moved me to a somewhat stronger belief in the Reagan thesis that it is generally better to rely on the private sector for some things than it is to rely on the government. The *Post* reported that for approximately forty-eight hours following the assassination attempt, the specially coded card that the president is supposed to use under certain conditions to authenticate nuclear strike orders was out of his control. Two government agencies were claiming that it belonged to them.

I might not have been moved toward the administration's position as strongly as I have been moved, were it not for the fact that the report on the president's lost or drifting card was made public at the same time that I was in the process of trying to get a supplemental American Express credit card.

American Express was very clear about its obligations and also about mine. I was to be called "The Basic Cardmember." If I didn't like anything that was going on, I was instructed to cut the card in half immediately and return both halves to American Express.

I was to be held responsible for anything done with the card. No other person, I was warned, was to use the card for any purpose— not for charging, not for identification, or for any other reason (picking teeth, screwdriving, scraping sleet off windshields, opening car doors, for example). If I relinquished physical possession, I would be responsible for everything done with the card by the holder.

I was admonished that I had agreed to notify American Express at once if the card was lost or stolen, or if I suspected it was being used or might be used without my permission.

American Express reserved the right to revoke the card if I were careless in the handling of it. Such is security in the private sector.

What of the government and its watchfulness over the president's card? According to the *Post*, at some point in the rush of events following the shooting of the president, an FBI agent got possession of the card. The president's special aide had run off with the mysterious black box. When the military aides tried to get the card from the FBI, it was denied them, under orders of the attorney general.

Officials identified as "knowledgeable" said that there was no loss of control, and no critical period, as a new card was issued. By whose authority, they did not say. Such easy issue of a new card would never have been tolerated by American Express.

As further assurance to the *Post*, the same knowledgeable officials, or others, said that in any case there was a duplicate of the president's card, held by someone in the Pentagon. President Reagan was reported to have been disturbed to learn of the duplicate. Under American Express procedures, he would have cut his card in two and sent it in.

To add to the confusion, "authoritative officials" went on to say that not only was there this one identical card, but that there were a number of cards with codes very close to that on the president's card—"unique cards," they were called, held in two lines, one running down through a series of officers in the Pentagon and another in the Cabinet, from Vice President Bush, the secretary of defense, and so on.

Just how these special cards might be used, or in what order or combination, was not revealed to the *Post*. Certainly such confusion, duplication, and proliferation of cards would not be tolerated by American Express. To paraphrase slightly the deathless words of Jack Valenti, former aide to President Lyndon Johnson, "We might all sleep better if American Express were in charge of the security of the code cards to be used to 'authenticate nuclear strike orders.' "

IS REFORM

SUCH A GOOD IDEA?

(*Washington Star*, APRIL 23, 1978)

The cry of "Reform the Bureaucracy" or "Reform the Civil Service" is as old as bureaucracy and civil service. It is a standard item in the catalog of demagoguery. President Jimmy Carter used it in the 1976 campaign with some success, according to the judgment of experts. He has followed that success with recommendations for an overall overhaul of the federal civil service.

His proposals have generally been approved, if not acclaimed. The *Washington Post* said that the president's plan is an excellent one, "on the whole." Whether the whole is greater than the sum of its parts remains to be seen. The government employee spokesmen are not so sure about the desirability of the parts. The *Post* also observed that, in presenting the nation with his plan for revising and reforming the civil service, President Carter did "one of the things he does best." The *Post* did not identify the other things, or the other thing, he does best.

Not surprisingly, a national business group, the Committee for Economic Development, has endorsed the Carter program. The CED ideas incorporated in the proposals are not shallow or fly-by-night. They are ideas, according to the CED, that "evolved over the past 35 years." Apparently ideas that have "evolved" are better than ideas that have come from reflection and observation. The evolutionary process, according to a CED spokesman, has not been left to chance or nature or time, but has been sustained by "in-depth research."

A major change recommended by the CED is that the Civil Service Commission be abolished and that it be replaced by two separate entities—one that will hire employees and another that will (among other things) fire them. This is supposed to be an application of business principles to government service. Government employee spokesmen have noted that they are not familiar with any business organization in which one authority hires workers and another fires them. This is, in any case, an innovative idea. And Alan Campbell, described as a chief administration "salesman" for change, is reported to be "delighted" with the CED statement. There is nothing like a delighted salesman.

The reform provides for a floating corps of administrators, to be called the Senior Executive Service, from which group administrators can be assigned wherever they are needed. They would represent in the civil service a trend that has already developed at the cabinet level. The outstanding example is Elliot Richardson, who (without pause or apology) has been moved, in no logical order, in and out of offices such as secretary of health, education, and welfare, secretary of defense, attorney general, secretary of commerce, ambassador to the United Kingdom, and special representative of the president for the Law of the Sea Conference. James Schlesinger is a close rival, having taken on (without pause for study or breath) defense, CIA, and energy.

Robert Strauss appears to be the current genius as utility fielder and designated hitter. Having been put in charge of trade problems, he came on strong with the reputation for being a hard bargainer. He may have been, and things might be worse if it hadn't been for Strauss. But the fact is that, either because of Strauss or despite him, the trade balance has worsened during his period of responsibility. Now he is to be put in charge of controlling inflation. One must question why the "floating administrator policy," which seems not to have worked well outside of the civil service, should now be incorporated into that service in the name of increased efficiency and effectiveness.

There are two basic questions to be raised about the Carter reforms. First: Is the civil service as ineffective as it is said to be? If the answer to the question is affirmative, a second question is: Do we want the civil service to be more effective than it is? The Internal Revenue Service, for example?

Perhaps President Carter and his associates and supporters should have read Mr. Dooley and reflected on his observations about reforms and reformers. "In th' first place," said Dooley, "tis a gr-reat mistake to think that annywan ra-aly wants to rayform. . . . An' that's thruer in politics thin annywhere else. But a rayformer don't see it. A rayformer thinks he was ilicted because he was a rayformer, win th' thruth iv th' matther is he was ilicted because no wan knew him. He's ilicted because th' people don't know him an' do know th' other la-ad. . . ."

This experience sustains the advice, regularly given by an experienced congressman, which was: "Never vote for anything which begins with 're'—reform, reorganization, recodification, resolutions." And since he was a Democrat, he added, "Republicans."

SPECIAL PROSECUTOR:

FALSELY ALLAYING DOUBT

(*Washington Star*, JULY 11, 1978)

During the years of controversy over civil rights legislation, there were proposals for a superior Supreme Court, a *Supreme* Supreme Court, to which cases decided in the Supreme Court would be appealed. It was a court that would have been, according to explanations given by its sponsors, above prejudice, above partisanship, above regionalism, above and beyond the corruption of intellect and will that besets even Supreme Court justices. Its wisdom would have been preternatural, just short of angelic.

In the same spirit, the Congress is now undertaking to purify the judicial process in another office. The House of Representatives is considering a bill, already passed by the Senate, to establish procedures for the appointment of a special prosecutor. This legislation modifies earlier proposals for a permanent special prosecutor.

There will be no permanent special prosecutor sitting in judgment, ready to go into action against high officials. Instead, the bill provides that if the attorney general has evidence that the president, vice president, or chairman of a presidential campaign has committed a crime involving a federal office or campaign, obstruction of justice, or perjury, he must ask a special three-judge court to appoint a special prosecutor. A special prosecutor would also be appointed if the attorney general believes that the president, the president's political party, or the attorney general himself has such an interest in a case that it is improper for the Justice Department to handle that case.

Once appointed, the special prosecutor could be removed by the attorney general for "extraordinary impropriety," or by the constitutional process of impeachment.

The justification given for the bill is Watergate, which was also the justification for passage of the Federal Election Campaign Act. In its first examination of that act, the Supreme Court held that it violated freedom of speech in two major respects and that it violated the constitutional provisions for separation of powers. Advocates of the act evidently thought that such violations were a small price to pay for purification.

The special prosecutor bill is an attempt to avoid the constitutional and political responsibility of the Congress to sit in judgment of the president and the executive branch. The attorney general of the United States, as an agent of the president, is responsible for enforcing the law against everyone in the country except the president. The president is subject to impeachment by the House and conviction by the Senate for "high crimes and misdemeanors" and also for felonies, which fall somewhere in between. This is a rational process, one that has satisfactorily met the test of history, even in the case of Watergate.

The Congress should not avoid its ultimate responsibility by defining conditions in which the appointment of a special prosecutor would be all but automatic. Moreover, it should not, as proposed in this instance, encourage the courts to become deeply involved in prosecution at such a high level of politics. The function of the courts is to judge, not to prosecute or to appoint prosecutors.

In any case, no matter how hard Congress may try, the element of politics will remain. Two political questions should be asked about the special prosecutor bill. The first is, "Who will appoint the attorney general?" And the second, "Who will appoint the three judges who in turn appoint a special prosecutor?" The attorney general, by tradition, will be a partisan appointee. The federal judges are where they are because of partisan support. No judge in recent history has been nominated by an independent president or confirmed by an independent, nonpartisan Congress.

Under a partisan system, no matter how many layers of partisan appointees are placed between the action and the actor, there will remain a whisper of doubt and suspicion. As a rule of government, it is better to place the area of doubt in range of judgment, rather than to pretend that it does not exist. It cannot be significantly reduced by a process that camouflages or obscures the fact that partisanship is built into the American political system.

FROM CLEARING TO CLEARING
WITH THE REAGAN
ADMINISTRATION

(Culpeper News, JANUARY 21, 1982)

As the Reagan administration nears the end of its first term, it has not shown any clear line of development or direction. It has not, however, been marked by contradictions or reversals of policy, as was the Carter administration. What we have had has been a sequence of happenings, one following the other in time, but not bound together by a consistent or orderly line of thought. Cohesiveness is provided by a set of overriding tenets, which are criticized as having failed in the past as guides to political, economic, and social progress. They are defended with the countering statement that they have not failed, but rather have not been honestly tried.

A partial list of these tenets follows:

1. The private sector always does things better than does the public sector.
2. Trust the open market to bring about desirable changes (e.g., small, efficient cars rather than large, wasteful ones).
3. Free enterprise is the only acceptable form of business organization.
4. The U.S. can only negotiate with the Russians from a position of strength, not one of parity.
5. Many, if not most, people who are out of work don't want to work.
6. Economic morality cannot be legislated, but private morality can be controlled and directed by law.
7. Competitiveness is the watchword.
8. Protectionism is the great threat to the economy.
9. Gold is the most reliable storehouse of value and, possibly, the best reserve behind a monetary and credit system, unless one follows the ways of Solomon and uses a copper standard.

Each time I see the president in a public place, or on television, I am reminded of my first meeting with him in what was billed as a debate on economic issues. It was before a group of business executives somewhere in New Jersey.

In making travel arrangements with the host group, I was asked whether I objected to flying in a helicopter from the New York airport to the scene of the meeting. I had no objection and subsequently was picked up at the airport and flown by helicopter across Manhattan, over the swamps of New Jersey, and then, for what seemed a long time, over heavy woods (it appeared to be a kind of jungle from the air), something I never suspected existed in New Jersey. At length, among the trees, I sighted a clearing. In it were tennis courts, a large clubhouse, what looked like a twenty-seven-hole golf course, and a marked helicopter landing pad. Although I could not see it from the air, I concluded that there was a road somewhere under cover of the trees, since there was a parking lot with automobiles.

We landed on the pad. I was taken to my room in the clubhouse, and eventually to the reception and dinner, which was followed by the debate.

There I met Ronald Reagan. He looked like his pictures. He smiled. He nodded and tilted his head.

Most of the phrases I remembered from the New Jersey meeting I heard again during the campaign, and hear now in presidential speeches and press conferences. The "welfare queen" received early notice. The description of the national debt, as dollar bills stitched together and stretching from the earth to the moon and back again, was included, as well as statistics on the volume and weight of paper used by the federal agencies.

I sensed that Ronald Reagan lived from one clearing, physical and intellectual, to another; that he was, or is, picked up and dropped down or out; that he goes on, with clear breaks, from one stop, physical or mental, to the next. Most of his language has been well tested over the years, decades; some for centuries. Clichés are not necessarily bad. Most of them, when first spoken or written, were considered to be wise observations. (Solomon made at least part of his reputation writing and collecting proverbs.) The right cliché in the right clearing may serve very well. And so we have gone from clearing to clearing.

WATERGATE TO IRANGATE

(1988)

The Irangate incident of the Reagan administration should have come as no surprise. It incorporated and demonstrated three disruptive patterns of behavior and belief that have come to bear upon the United States government during recent administrations.

The first is the concept of the "inner ring." C. S. Lewis says it is a most dangerous concept in that very good men will do bad things once they believe they have a special role that exempts them from the ordinary rules of conduct. They imagine they are pursuing, in the public interest, a higher purpose. Having accepted their election or selection, those in the inner ring—like Oliver North, John

Poindexter, and others—modify the rules to fit their purposes. In a way they are not very different from Oliver Cromwell, when he answered questions about pride's purge and the execution of the king by saying, "Be not too critical of God's ways, perhaps there was no other way."

The second element is the *"Murder in the Cathedral* principle," used in Irangate and Watergate. Archbishop Thomas à Becket was murdered because the knights, although they were not told to perform the act, were certain that the king wanted the cleric killed, and that he would be pleased by their actions. This is comparable to Admiral Poindexter's statement that he knew what the president thought and proceeded to act on that basis. In the same manner, one of the Watergate operatives said that he would not have done what he had done, had he not thought that President Nixon wanted the deed done and would approve it. Nixon apparently did want the dirty tricks, did approve them, and sacrificed a part of his presidency because he defended the acts.

The third pattern or trend, one that has been growing slowly and subtly in recent decades, is the use of corporations or corporate officials as agents in questionable government operations that are kept secret from the public and, in many cases, from Congress. Harold Geneen revealed the working principle in congressional hearings held when he was president of International Telephone and Telegraph. He was asked why he, as president of his company, had approached the U.S. government asking it to transfer money to the CIA in order to finance operations that ITT wanted. He responded that it seemed only fair, since the CIA had transferred money—government money—to ITT in order to have that company carry out projects for the government. The Reagan administration has appealed to corporations and to individuals—and evidently also to other governments—to help finance projects not wholly approved by the public or by Congress. Accepting such assignments is an easy step for multinational or international corporations, which generally act as though they were independent of any national sovereignty.

When concepts such as these are accepted, Irangate should not be surprising. The inner ring is a concept based on the view that certain special persons are, and should be, above the law. The desire to please the king makes no allowances for law. Only the king matters. And the rogue multinational exists outside the context of nations, constitutions, order, and civility.

A SELF-FORGIVING PROPHECY

(Culpeper News, APRIL 17, 1980)

A new spirit of forgiveness, principally of self, is becoming a mark of American politics. This trend is clearly contrary to the earlier tradition of American politics, a tradition that persisted and went unchallenged well into the second half of this century.

According to the previously accepted rules, politicians were held responsible for their own mistakes and also for the mistakes and faults of former and current members of their own parties. For years Democrats held Republican presidential and congressional candidates accountable for the administration of Herbert Hoover. Adlai

Stevenson, in his campaigns for the presidency, had to answer for the very limited corruption of the Truman administration.

The first evidence of the new spirit appeared in the Eisenhower campaign. With Eisenhower, the issue was not one of forgiving him for past political failings, because he had no political record of his own and no record of identification with any political party. Rather, it was that of establishing his political innocence, so that he could not be held responsible for anything that might happen, or not happen, in his administration.

The new trend was first tested by the Nixon fund case. After Richard Nixon's "Checkers" speech, in which Nixon offered to forgive himself (an offer not quite acceptable), Eisenhower pronounced Nixon forgiven, and the campaign proceeded to a successful termination. This may well have been the critical point in the move away from the established practice of harsh political judgment, although as long as Nixon was involved politically, a clean break with the early practice was never quite possible. He could never quite carry off self-forgiveness. In explaining his part in Watergate, he made a halfhearted attempt when he said that he was responsible but that "we" were all to blame.

The great leap forward into the peaceable kingdom of political non-guilt came with the candidacy of Jimmy Carter. Carter took care of much of his past by being reborn and experiencing the freedom of forgiveness. Subsequently he has been forgiving of himself and, with some reservation, of others. But he has not always allowed to others the power of self-forgiveness that he has exercised in his own behalf. In his well-publicized *Playboy* interview of 1976, he expressed the confident belief that he was forgiven for the lust in his heart, and he went on to say that he was prepared to forgive carnal sinners. In dealing with the issue of amnesty for draft resisters, President Carter rejected the proposal of amnesty and opted for pardoning them. Pardoning, he said, implied that they had been guilty of something and therefore could be forgiven, but not by themselves.

Gerald Ford, when appearing before a congressional committee before the vote on his nomination for the vice presidency, asked Congress to forget or forgive him his voting record over the years because, he said, he had represented Grand Rapids, Michigan. He never explained why representing Grand Rapids established grounds for leniency.

As the 1980 presidential campaign moves along, forgiveness, especially of self, is running strongly. President Carter does not ask for forgiveness for his failure or for his reversals of position. He assumes it. The income-tax laws are not, as he said in his campaign, "a disgrace to the human race." Former foreign policy advisors Clark Clifford, Averill Harriman, and Henry Cabot Lodge, denounced as a group in the 1976 campaign, are now consulted, with appropriate publicity and no apologies.

Ronald Reagan blames his informants for errors about the size of the Kennedy tax reduction of 1964, for misstatements about Vietnam veterans and the GI bill for education, and walks away free.

And John Anderson, as a potential independent candidate, is heavily into self-exoneration. In answer to a question as to his most serious political mistake, he declares or confesses that it was his vote for the Tonkin Gulf Resolution. Such frankness merits forgiveness and forgetfulness.

Anderson has also acknowledged and done a kind of public penance for having introduced and advocated an amendment to the Constitution of the United States declaring that this nation is a Christian nation and providing that, except under special conditions, only Christians could hold high offices—the presidency, in Congress, and on the federal bench.

Forgiveness could become the dominant consideration in future presidential campaigns. Instead of debates between candidates, the League of Women Voters, sustained by the major networks, might present forgiveness contests, with the rival presidential candidates competing to show how much more forgiving, of self and of others, each one is. Thus may the Scripture be fulfilled that "to those who have sinned greatly much is forgiven."

A GOOD AND

BECOMING EXIT

(1988)

A truly good actor, it is said, is marked by his or her exits. At best they should be made such that, although the leaving may not have been noticed, the absence that follows is.

When Harold Macmillan died last month, the former prime minister of the United Kingdom took to his grave a singular distinction. He was the last prominent Western head of government to resign over a matter of principle. Though other factors (such as his ill health, Tory party divisions, and the Profumo scandal) had dimmed his will to govern, his failure to secure British membership in the Common Market rankled most. He had not lost a vote in the House of Commons; he had not lost his seat in a general election; yet he felt he could not in conscience continue to lead Great Britain. His subsequent career, though obscure, was wholly useful. Most recently Macmillan, as Lord Stockton, was an admonisher against current Thatcher policies, which he felt were demeaning to Tory tradition and, worse, likely to lead to the defeat of the party in the next election.

Other ministers of the Crown have resigned, both subsequently and previously, because they disapproved of government policy. The most recent was Michael Heseltine, former minister of defense under Margaret Thatcher. He objected to her plan to sell a British helicopter manufacturer to an American firm rather than to a European consortium. Jeffrey Archer, a member of Parliament and a novelist of no great distinction but of great commercial impact, more recently resigned as chairman of the Tory party over a reputed, but unproven, sexual scandal. He was not, however, a minister.

In the United States, sexual conduct seems to have little bearing on politics, or on political resignation. Financial dealings of questionable legality and morality are more often causes for resignation, and are sometimes followed by court proceedings and prison sentences. The usual defense is that the person accused believes he or she deserves the blame, but should not be held responsible. Businessmen, when under similar pressure to resign, more commonly say that they are responsible but not to blame. In both politics and business, the underlying assumption seems to be that unless one is both responsible and deserving of blame, somehow one is not guilty.

Officers of government below elected and cabinet rank have less occasion to depart than their superiors, if only because their responsibilities are lesser. When finally motivated to act, public officials who leave an administration whose position they can no longer support usually go quietly. They have been known to obscure their real reasons for leaving with explanations about health, family problems, or the need to earn money for educating their children. In the fifties and sixties, the fact that their corporate pensions would be in jeopardy used to be mentioned frequently. Nowadays, either private pension rules are more favorable to those who undertake government service, or else the fashion in excuses has changed—wanting to have more time with one's children tends to be today's popular reason.

Some stay on in service and, to all appearances, continue to support a policy of which they later say they did not approve. As time runs on, more of the persons who seemed to support the Vietnam War, and who stood against those who opposed the war, are saying that they really were against the war—or at least did not believe in it. Robert McNamara and Walter Mondale are prominent examples.

Others stay on and try to present their views from within, hoping that they can be more effective than if they left the citadel of power and joined, or attempted to lead, those outside the walls. George Ball evidently accepted this role in the Johnson administration and functioned as the devil's advocate on Vietnam. There is a prejudice against the devil's advocate, since he is cast as one representing the bad side of a good cause.

Others may stay on and disagree publicly, at least as long as allowed to do so. When General Douglas MacArthur, in command of our military effort in Korea, chose this course, President Truman responded by dismissing MacArthur. Watergate Special Prosecutor Archibald Cox met a similar fate in the Nixon administration.

Officials of high reputation may leave quietly and be silent forever. In unusual circumstances, silence itself can be construed as protest. Sir Thomas More, who left his position as chancellor of England when he could no longer support Henry VIII, went silently. But as playwright Robert Bolt reports it in *A Man for All Seasons*, Thomas Cromwell, Henry's chief secretary, complained that "this silence is bellowing up and down Europe." More was beheaded.

Other officials may leave in violent protest. There is no good American example: One must turn to Samson for a clear illustra-

tion. A political prisoner blinded by the Ph
son, as the Scriptures say, ". . . took hold (
upon which the house stood, and on whic
he bowed himself with all his might, an(
lords, and upon the people that were therein

There is another way out; namely, to l(
ment of reasons for leaving. This is the w
American politics. There are strong cultur.
for this. First, although it is perhaps time 1
no tradition of resignation for purpose in A1
is in England, other European democraci(
and Israel. Second, the structure of parliame
little room for a dissident in a functioning
our system the concept of cabinet memb(
to a president, makes it easier to accept th

There are also strong forces in American
dissent and against resignation. Loyalty to
Thus, Governor Nelson Rockefeller receiv(
the Republican nomination in 1968 becau;
port the party's nominee, Senator Barry G
ever, most of the candidates for the Demo(
nomination in 1968—even, or especially,
war in Vietnam—were quick to say that
party's nominee no matter who he might
form would be.

Besides party loyalty, another inhibiting
usually propagated by the administration in
leaves is a quitter. A term from cattlehan
by Lyndon Johnson, saying that a departi
run," might depict the attitude of most p
dinates, whether on or off the ranch.

In each case the person or persons invc
to act with dignity and integrity, as relate
hold or the seriousness of their disagreem
a useful example when he resigned as pre;

, rather than continue as spokesman for an administration
cated "disinformation."

fficials may stay on and murmur against presidents and
n the gates and porticoes, at dinners and at cocktail par-
offer high-level leaks to columnists and editors. This is
reprehensible, though most frequent, response.

ry of State George Shultz has been tested. A person in
fice is never wholly free to keep private his views on vital
atters. That person must accept those times when the public
rrides personal considerations, and when loyalty to party,
ice, or even to a president should be set aside.

e when resignations with explanations are both right and
y for the public good comes infrequently. But when it does
e statesman should sit up and be heard.

BY THEIR WORDS

SHALL YOU KNOW THEM

(Report of the Commission, Miller Center,

University of Virginia, 1987)

The Scriptures sayeth, "By their works shall you know them." A person I know, a student of both language and politics, says that this word from the Good Book does not apply to politics at the level of presidential campaigning and of performance in office. In judging presidential candidates and presidents in office, he gives precedence to another scriptural test, "In the beginning was the Word," as a better and earlier indicator of what to expect.

Therefore, he argues, words of presidents and of potential presidents must be closely evaluated, not as the substance of speeches, but simply as words—nouns, verbs, prepositions, pronouns, adjectives, adverbs, and so on.

There were indications of things to come, he noted, in the increasingly frequent use of the possessive pronoun *my*, and its broader application, by President Lyndon Johnson following his landslide victory in 1964. Instead of referring to the Cabinet as "the Cabinet," giving some credit to the Senate for having confirmed its members, he called it "my Cabinet." The Democratic party became for him "my party," a claim challenged in 1968. He referred to the vice president as "my vice president," evidently unaware of the sensitivity one should use in the application of the possessive. Charles Péguy, a French philosopher, noted in a criticism of the modern world early in this century that the necessary distinctions in the use of the possessive *my* had been lost, and it was applied indiscriminately to property, dogs and cats, wives and children, and even God. The extreme application of the word, by President Johnson, was demonstrated when at an airbase he directed an airman to move a helicopter. When the airman replied that he could not do so without orders from his immediate commanding officer, the president is reported to have said, "They're *my* helicopters."

President Richard Nixon may have been more discriminating than Johnson in the use of *my*, but he was inclined to use more intimate and absolute possession—indicating words, namely, *we* and *our*, in a kind of mystical or metaphysical sense, making us one with him.

There had been earlier indications of this disposition on the part of President Nixon. In his speech accepting the Republican nomination for the presidency in 1968, he used *we* approximately ninety times and *I* only about fifty-five times. Four years later, again accepting the nomination of his party, he was a little stronger into *I*, using that word about sixty times and relying on *we* some fifty times.

Gerald Ford, accepting the 1976 nomination, and evidently still thinking or speaking in the Nixon tradition, used *I* only nine times and *we* twenty-five times. Both Nixon and Ford were probably not familiar with Mark Twain's observation that no one had a right to use the collective *we* unless he was "the King of England" (or, if a she, the Queen), "the Archbishop of Canterbury" (or, one assumes, the Pope), "or someone with a tapeworm."

Nixon, as the linguistic scholar also noted, was attracted to predicate adjectives, in the mode of Muhammad Ali's best-remembered quotation, "I am the greatest." Nixon used a few adjectives often, such as *first, best, biggest,* and especially *greatest.* In his first acceptance speech, he used *greatest,* or a variation of it, at least twenty times.

The Carter campaign and subsequent administration were marked not by the dominance of any pronouns or adjectives, but by adverbs. This penchant for adverbs was indicated early in the campaign, when, in one of the first interviews, the candidate was asked whether he had been immersed at his baptism. He answered, "totally." On another occasion, he said that he remembered "avidly," something not commonly done, and promised to evolve and "consummate" a foreign policy "openly" and "frankly."

President Jimmy Carter was inclined to turn to adverbs in difficult situations. One of his most adverb-laden statements was one given following the taking of the American hostages by the government of Iran. A partial list of adverbs used (some more than once) includes *directly, recently, completely, obviously, primarily, fairly, possibly, historically, actually, exactly,* and *presently.* The "what was" and the "what was to be done" (or not to be done) were smothered by the hows, whens, wheres, and whys of the adverbs, making the Carter administration essentially an adverbial administration, with degrees and shadings of the verbs more important than the nouns and verbs themselves.

Walter Mondale's speech, as a candidate for the vice presidency and for the presidency, was distinguished by his use of adjectives. Thus, during the 1980 campaign to reelect Carter and Mondale, the vice president, in one sentence—and, one assumes, in one breath— described President Carter as "honest, caring, intelligent, brilliant, committed, courageous, experienced,"—almost too many adjectives for either a sentence or a person to carry. It is excusable for a vice president to go to extremes in describing the president, since the role of the vice president is primarily one of modifying—somewhat in the way a tennis pro functions, not so much to improve his students as to make them look good and feel satisfied with themselves.

The "dominant adjective" showed up in Mondale speeches in his own campaign for the presidency in 1984. Then he said that the Russian leaders were "cynical and dangerous," that the Soviet military buildup was "relentless" and went well beyond their "defensive" needs, and that the buildup posed a "direct" challenge to "Western" security. He proposed a "coherent" strategy; an "enhanced" NATO; "sensible," "mutual," and "verifiable" arms control; an "improved" Minuteman missile; an "accelerated" submarine missile program; more "conventional" capability, "negotiated" arms reductions; a "comprehensive" test-ban treaty; "tougher" restraints on nuclear proliferation; a "coherent" strategy. He said he was looking for a "crucial" consensus and added that our interests should be "defined, feasible, defensible," subjected to "independent" scrutiny, and "alert" to "regional" history. And he asked Gary Hart, "Where's the beef?"

The Reagan language is difficult to analyze on the basis of parts of speech, since he speaks largely in clichés, some of which, when originally spoken, must have seemed well spoken. And so the campaign of 1984 ran out, a contest essentially between the cliché and the adjective, with the cliché winning.

No clear language patterns have emerged in the presidential races thus far. We may have to wait for the showdown campaign of the nominees of each party. Most, if not all, of the Democratic candidates have emphasized *I*, trying to distinguish their own candidacies from those of other Democratic candidates. Among the Republicans, Robert Dole has been the strongest *I* person, whereas George Bush is markedly into the use of *we*, meaning himself and President Reagan. Jack Kemp seemed to be claiming that he was a part of the *we*, to which President Reagan belonged, and Pat Robertson, who had been fairly intimate with God (in almost a *We* relationship), tried with little success in the campaign to temporarily break off those ties and go it on his own.

POLITICAL NICKNAMES

(Progressive Review, NOVEMBER 1, 1984)

The two candidates on the 1984 Republican ticket appear to be running with their given first names intact. President Reagan, as a candidate in 1980, did use the familiar form "Ronnie" some, but he seems to have chosen the more dignified "Ronald" in running as an incumbent.

George Bush has not used a familiar or diminutive form of George. "Georgie," in any case, would probably be rejected by public relations experts as weak or unfamiliar, even as feminine.

Geraldine Ferraro is occasionally called "Gerry" by the media, and that name shows up on placards at Democratic rallies. She is most often, however, called "Geraldine" in press reports. More attention has been given to surnames in her case.

The name that is used to identify, or characterize, the Democratic presidential candidate has, it seems, received more and more attention as the campaign has gone on. One of the rallying cries at the Democratic convention was, "We want Fritz." In the early primaries, the nickname could not be used freely because there was a second Democratic candidate who was better known as "Fritz" than was Walter Mondale. That candidate was Ernest Hollings.

With Hollings out of the race, "Fritz" could be claimed singularly. Recently I received a letter over the signature of candidate Mondale's wife, Joan, asking for a campaign contribution. The substance of the appeal was pretty much the standard material of campaign appeals, with two exceptions. First, it made a special point of how the campaign had drawn the Mondale family closer, a development that Joan seemed to think was worthy of consideration; and second, it was marked by repeated references to the presidential candidate as "Fritz"—ten times in three pages of text.

Walter Mondale, evidently, has been "Fritz" to his family and to his close friends for a long time and understandably could prefer that name when among intimate associates to, say, "Wally" or even "Walt."

For public use, I have thought "Walter" or "Walt" preferable. The Walters and Walts I have known in history, literature, and real life have generally been solid, reliable types: for example, Walt Whitman, Walter Johnson, Walter Krengel, Walter Cronkite, Walter Scott, Walther von der Vogelweide.

"Walter" also lends itself to alliterative slogans better than "Fritz," which is essentially limited to a phrase like "Fighting Fritz." Walter fits easily into statements such as, "We want Walter," or "Win with Walter," or even "Warlike Walter," to go with the recent trend in Mondale's rhetoric toward stronger, harsher, and more militant words such as *savage, trash, assault, clobber, sock it to them,* and *kill.*

From the defensive point of view, the use of "Walter," or a variant of it, would be as good a choice as "Fritz." Potential presidents must anticipate the longer-range historical possibilities, the danger of having a labeling adjective attached to a presidential name. (Aethelred II, the English king about the year A.D. 1000, was branded "Aethelred the Unready" and carries that name in the historical record today.)

My attitude toward the name "Fritz" may be negative not because of any historical or literary association, but because of my experience in my hometown. Nicknames were common, but not ordinary. They were, as I look back, almost art forms. The Werner family, for example, had one son named Gregory, who was called "Dutch"; another, Raphael, who was known as "Rats"; and one baptized Elmer, who carried two names used interchangeably by townspeople, either "Nick" or "Candy."

Another family, with the surname Manuel, had a son named Andrew, who was called "Span"; an Aloysius who carried the name "Stub" although he was quite tall; an Edwin called "Pat"; and another son called Louis, whose nickname was "Boom." The two daughters were Evelyn, called "Putch," and Gertrude, who was known as "Tamp" or "Tampy."

In all this range of nicknames, in a population largely German, among whom the name Frederick was very popular, the nickname "Fritz" never took hold. The shortened form, "Fred," was used. I had a cousin "Fred." His son was called not "Junior" or "Fritz," but "Freddie." There were a few named "Fritzie," but they were different, "Fritzie" Nistler, for example, the best whistler in the county, or girls.

"Fritz" was allowed for an occasional stranger who might pass through town. But locally it was reserved largely, if not exclusively, as a name for horses. My father owned a horse called "Fritz." He said it was the "best and brightest" horse he ever owned.

POPULAR ILLNESSES:
JUST PART OF
THE PRESIDENT'S JOB

(*Culpeper News*, SEPTEMBER 12, 1985)

A number of pundits have declared that Ronald Reagan, through his making public and available to the media details of the condition of his colon, has "done a lot for" cancer. I do not know whether these writers had firm evidence of what the president had done, were assuming good results, or, rather, were merely justifying their excessive and detailed press coverage.

The theme was picked up and extended to credit Rock Hudson with having "done a lot for" AIDS by making public his condition. Others in the media went back to credit Betty Ford for "having done a lot for" breast cancer, and for alcoholism.

This disposition in public figures, including presidents and their wives, to go public with their physical disabilities is a relatively new development. President Franklin Roosevelt's disability was publicly known, but treated with decent respect. Pictures of him in his wheelchair were rare, and the public was spared pictures of his struggling to assume a standing position behind a rostrum.

Harry Truman, if he had any serious physical ailments, kept quiet about them. He may have done some good for bourbon, and for cussing, but none for painkillers or antacid potions or tablets. His wife, Bess, was similarly reserved about her health.

The public did hear a lot about ileitis during President Dwight Eisenhower's bout with that affliction. Some persons may be more ready now than before to admit to having ileitis, although there was never any stigma or social significance attached to the disease. Commentators were not moved to say that the president had "done a lot for" ileitis. So, too, his heart attack seemed to be accepted as more or less standard.

President John Kennedy did not make public reports on the state of his health, or on the medicines and physical therapy he was taking. He did publicly relate the use of his rocking chair to his bad back, and, possibly, by doing so "did something for" rocking chairs. Reporters with medical interests during the Kennedy administration seemed to be satisfied to report on obstetrics and pediatrics.

President Lyndon Johnson was restrained. He seemed quite pleased with his gallbladder operation, and willingly showed his scar. No one claimed then or since that his exposure did much for gallstones or for the treatment of diseases of the gallbladder.

By contrast, President Richard Nixon played down his phlebitis, possibly missing a chance of "doing a lot for" the disorder, which seems to attract little attention.

Jimmy Carter, as the Democratic nominee, asked for medical reports from all of his vice-presidential applicants and made public his own problem of hemorrhoids. It was not noted at the time that he was doing much, if anything, for hemorrhoids, but some evidence has accumulated that suggests that he did have some impact on public attitudes toward his ailment.

Hemorrhoids are not yet talked about in social situations, but the most noticeable change in attitude toward the problem is in television advertising. Until relatively recently, hemorrhoid ads were restricted to afternoon soap operas and late-night television programs.

But ads offering relief, if not cure, of hemorrhoids are now appearing more frequently during prime-time television—and also, I have noted, during the "CBS Evening News." In Walter Cronkite's reign as anchorman, it was common to include, at or near the end of his news broadcast, an advertisement for Ex-Lax, after which Walter would say, in his reassuring tone, "That's the way it is."

A PLACE FOR LIBERALS TO HIDE

(New Republic, June 13, 1983)

Liberals have been on the defensive in recent years, under attack from conservatives and other "liberals," for the most part self-defined.

The first public challenge to my "liberalism" came in a debate appearance, several years ago, with William Rusher, then an editor of the National Review.

Mr. Rusher, the publisher of the magazine *National Review*, is a self-declared conservative. He is also precise about the definition and use of words. In the course of meeting with me, he repeatedly made the point that he and his ideological compatriots are not "neoconservatives," but that they belong rather to the "new right." Since I had made no attempt to categorize Mr. Rusher, I could not quite understand his anxiety about "neoconservatism," and anticipated that possibly he was going to make further distinctions, possibly with respect to "plio-conservatism" or even "mio-conservatism." As it turned out, Mr. Rusher seemed to have some objection to the linguistic impurity of mixing the Greek *neo* with the Latinate *conservative,* but this objection was moderate and almost incidental. The serious basis of his distinction was historical. "Neoconservatives," he said, lacked historical purity. The persons so labeled, either by themselves or by others, were former "liberals," he said, whereas the persons admitted to his group, the "new right," had always been "right," as distinct both from the "old right," which he did not define but implied might sometimes have been wrong, and from the "neoconservatives," who, in their previous incarnation as liberals, had never been "right." I was eager to let the whole matter pass as a quarrel among the various phyla of "conservatives," but then Mr. Rusher insisted on calling me a "liberal."

I objected, going back to an old contention of mine that the word *liberal* should never be used as a noun, only as an adjective. Thus, one may be a liberal democrat or a liberal Republican, a liberal Catholic or a liberal Presbyterian, but never a pure "liberal." This was a posture I had taken up in the late 1950s, when "liberal," having just achieved status as a noun, was being festooned with derogatory prefixes. J. Edgar Hoover, in those days, was warning against what he called the "pseudo-liberals," William F. Buckley, Jr., was writing about the "illogical-liberals," and others spoke and wrote about the "egghead-liberals," the "crypto-liberals," and so on.

In the days and weeks following my encounter with Mr. Rusher, I began to notice that the word *liberal* was again being subjected to prefix transplant operations. The crucial term in this process first surfaced in the "liberal" press (especially *The Washington*

Monthly and the *New Republic)*, and then was picked up in the "conservative" press, beginning with an editorial in *The Wall Street Journal* entitled "The Neo-Libs." The *Journal*'s distinction paralleled one made in an earlier article in *The American Spectator*, in January 1982. That article referred to New York City's Mayor Edward Koch as "once a liberal purist." Obviously the author meant to label Koch as "once a pure liberal," in the old style. Strictly speaking, a "liberal purist" would be a purist who was rather loose in questions of purity, and thus would be too lax to practice what *The American Spectator* article referred to as "undiluted liberalism." In this article, Mr. Koch is also called "a liberal with sanity," or, one might say, a "sane liberal," as distinguished from, possibly, an "insane liberal."

Both *The American Spectator* and the *Journal* divided the "neo-liberals" into two classes. One is made up of "traditional liberals," who were once what William Rusher would probably call "the old left" (comparable to the "old right" of his world), but have changed some. Yet they do not want to be called the "new left," as Rusher's associates gladly call themselves the "new right," partly because the old "new left," which scarcely exists anymore, used to be so disdainful of "liberals" of any type, but especially "bourgeois liberals." The other division of "neo-liberals," the Koch type, includes persons such as Senator Paul Tsongas of Massachusetts, who called himself a "new liberal" and a "revisionist liberal," and Senator Gary Hart of Colorado, who distinguished himself as a "pragmatic liberal." Both of these wings, I gather, are agreed on one point, namely, that they are different from "unreconstructed liberals."

In the midst of all of these fine tunings, I have concluded that for some time to come, the word *liberal* will be useless as a means of political communication and should be allowed to rest, pending rehabilitation.

What has happened to that good word is roughly comparable to what happened to the goat in history. From humble and useful beginnings, as a source of milk and meat, the goat gradually worked its way up through various orders of religious symbolism to the exalted position of scapegoat, bearing the sins of the tribe into the desert, or over the cliff. From there, the goat began a slow decline, and finally lost even its most ardent supporters, who began to question its powers, allowing it to attend only disreputable revels. The goat finally became the object of derision, eating garbage, used as the image for lewd old men, and blamed for the loss of baseball games.

The word *liberal* has not fallen quite so low. What began as a modest and useful adjective became a noun, the equivalent of deification. It can be saved, possibly even restored to good standing. But until it recovers, those who need a covering term might consider the name of a new group still in the early stages of organization. They are "the neos" — pure, simple, pristine, unmodified, in no historical or ideological context.

The rules of the new order are simple. First, its members must resist any attempt to attach any modifier, whether prefix or suffix, to the key word, *neo.* Second, they must be willing to cast off fixed ideas in politics, economics, and the social field in general every seven years. The seven-year period has been chosen for sound reasons. There is strong biblical support for the number seven. Pagan and Christian civilizations alike have recognized the power of seven. Physiologists say that the chemicals and other physical material of the human body change completely every seven years. Moreover, because seven is a prime number, the "neos" have a running start on survival. As in the case of the seventeen-year locust, the likelihood that natural predators will appear in dangerous numbers is scant. Because of this principle, the "neos" may propose one seven-year term for the president of the United States.

The only organized group that has applied for acceptance into the "neos" is the Pigeon-Kicking Society of America, which has only two members and has one rule of action — that to remain an active member, one must kick a pigeon once every seven years, or submit proof of having made a serious effort to do so.

THE HIGH COST OF

"NEW MEANING"

(*Washington Star*, MARCH 5, 1978)

Giving new meaning to the vice presidency — a concern of the last quarter-century of American government — was expected to accomplish two principal goals. It was supposed to be good for the country and it was supposed to provide a happier, more fulfilling life for the vice president.

Giving new meaning to the vice presidency may be good for the country in the long run. In the short run, the benefits have not yet been demonstrated, although there is hope — perhaps even promise — that the new meaning may be demonstrated as beneficial in this administration.

As to the goal of making the office more meaningful so that vice presidents would be happier, have a greater sense of fulfillment, and bear their cross more patiently, again the record is mixed, but for the most part unsatisfactory. The record does not indicate that, even with the new meaning and accompanying responsibilities, the vice presidents from Nixon through Johnson, Humphrey, Agnew, and Rockefeller were particularly happy or satisfied. Gerald Ford seemed content with whatever meaning the office held for him, but his term was too short for full testing.

The effect that the vice president's residence has on the nature of the office, and the performance and satisfaction of the vice president and his family, is now in its first full term of testing. Nelson Rockefeller was not fully tested. Although he had the vice-presidential residence available, at least for a short time, and even went so far as to move his Max Ernst bed into the mansion, he himself never moved in. He was, in any case, adequately housed; and he seemed to sense that his tenure as vice president was limited.

It is clear that, as the effort to give new meaning to the office has continued, the cost of that effort has increased in each succeeding administration.

The last "old meaning" vice president was Alben Barkley, who served from 1949 to 1953. According to government figures, Barkley received a salary that averaged slightly less than $30,000 a year. His expense allowance averaged less than $50,000 a year.

During the eight years that Richard Nixon served as vice president, the office received "new meaning." Whereas the vice-presidential salary remained relatively constant at about $33,000 a year, the allowance for running the office increased from $55,000 a year in 1953 to $112,000 in 1960, Nixon's last year as vice president.

Although it was publicly reported during the 1960 campaign that Lyndon Johnson would have new and special assignments as vice president, expenses did not reflect such changes. Johnson's salary remained constant at $35,000; while his office allowance increased from $112,000 in 1961 to $128,000 in 1963, that did little more than take care of inflation.

A great leap forward, or upward, took place when the allowance increased from $137,000 a year in 1965 to $235,000 a year in 1968.

In the first four years of the Nixon administration, the expense allowance rose from $246,000 in 1969 to $415,000 in 1972. (Those were the years during which Spiro Agnew was putting his mark on the vice presidency and the administration.)

From 1973 to the end of 1976, a period during which three different persons held the vice-presidential office, the allowance rose from $430,000 a year to $584,000 a year.

In 1977, in addition to the vice president's salary of $71,000, $615,000 was allocated for office expenses. In 1978, the salary is pegged at $75,000 and the expense allowance has risen to $687,000. It is projected that the office will receive $723,000 for expenses in 1979. In addition, the official residence of the vice president, which cost $91,000 in 1977, will cost an estimated $129,000 in 1979.

In another category called "special assistance to the president," vice-presidential expenses, which previously were carried in appropriations to departments and agencies but are now separated from those appropriations, rose from $700,000 year in 1971 to an estimated $1,327,000 in 1978.

Summing up: In Alben Barkley's day, the vice presidency cost about $80,000 a year. Today it costs $2,210,000 a year.

The time has come to say of the vice president, as Aunt Mabel (in a poem by William Stafford) said of her Senator:

He's a brilliant man,
But we didn't elect him that much.

ADVICE TO THE NEWLY

ELECTED, OR TEN COMMANDMENTS

FOR NEW MEMBERS

OF CONGRESS

(*Culpeper News*, DECEMBER 11, 1980)

Newly elected members of Congress will soon be introduced to Washington and to their new duties and responsibilities. Both parties offer help to their party members. Various foundations, institutes, and institutions will hold seminars for new members and brief them. The press will make its recommendations, and the special-interest groups (as defined by Common Cause) and the public-interest groups (also as defined by Common Cause) make suggestions both procedural and substantive.

I will not take up the substantive matters, the subject of party platforms and of campaigns, matters for legislative action. Instead, I offer advice on procedures and suggestions for behavior.

New members will be asked to advocate reforms and reorganizations of various kinds. They will be told that critical to their success is a dedicated, hardworking staff; that it is vital they know the rules of procedure of the body to which they have been elected; that they should maintain a near-perfect, if not perfect, attendance record; that Washington politics is a very complicated process, requiring continuous attention and high intelligence; that what seems to be complicated is in fact very simple; and that what appears to be simple is very complicated. Some of their counselors will see the seniority system, as it still operates, as the enemy of good legislative procedures. New members will be told on the one hand to stand on principle, not to be afraid to be the single opponent of a measure or a policy, if integrity and principle are involved. On the other hand, they will be urged to stick with the party, to be loyal, to learn how to compromise, to adhere to the middle way, and especially to try to have good relationships with the press, founded on mutual trust. And so on.

Most of this advice will be bad. I have compiled a set of ten commandments that, if observed by new members, will protect them from most of the bad advice they have been given and will be given.

I

Vote against anything introduced with "re-" — reforms, reorganizations, recodifications, and especially resolutions.

II

Do not have a perfect, or near-perfect, attendance record. If a new member has an attendance record better than 80 percent, there is reason to believe that he or she has been wasting time answering roll calls and quorum calls. A member who has been in office for several terms should work his attendance record down to 65 or 70 percent.

III

Do not worry too much about rules or procedures or spend much time trying to learn them. The Senate rules are simple enough to be learned, but they are seldom honored in practice. The House rules are generally applied, but they are too complicated to be worth mastering. The parliamentarian is always available.

IV

Beware of a staff that is too efficient. Never trust a staff member who regularly gets to the office before you do and who stays after you leave.

V

Don't worry too much about intelligence. Remember that politics is much like coaching professional football — those who are most successful are just smart enough to understand the game, but not smart enough to lose interest.

VI

Don't knock the seniority system; you may have seniority sooner than you anticipate. Moreover, the practice of having senior members assume responsibility as committee chairpersons, although not a rational process, does, as Gilbert Chesterton observed of the ancient practice of having the oldest son of a king accede to the throne, "save a lot of trouble."

VII

Don't, unless the issue is overwhelming, be the only one, or one of a few, who is right about it, especially if it is an issue that will not go away. It is difficult to say to one's colleagues in Congress, "I am sorry I was right. Please forgive me." They won't.

VIII

Remember that the worst accidents occur in or near the middle of the road.

IX

Do not respond to the appeal of "party loyalty." This can be the last defense of political rascals. Remember that those who "go along" do not always "get along."

X

As Ed Leahy, noted reporter of the Chicago *Daily News*, said to me soon after I arrived in Congress thirty years ago, "Never trust the press."

FEVER TO DO GOOD

CONSUMES U.S.

(*Rushville Republican*, MARCH 17, 1979)

"There is so great a fever on goodness," says the Duke in Shakespeare's *Measure for Measure*, "that the dissolution of it must cure it."

The fever on doing good, or of trying to make others do good, has now gone through the executive branch of the government. The president and the vice president have disclosed their financial holdings, as well as their physical disabilities. The cabinet members have disclosed their financial affairs. Other top-ranking officials, under a new law that will take effect in July, will be required to list their financial holdings so as to disclose any possibility of conflict of interest.

The interest of the purifiers has now turned to the judiciary. Under the Constitution, federal judges are nominated by the president and confirmed by the Senate. This procedure was settled on, after long debate in the Constitutional Convention, as the best way to ensure judicial independence. Proposals to have judges elected directly were rejected. Proposals to have them appointed by the president, without any confirmation by the Congress, were also considered and rejected, as were other variations. To further ensure the independence of the judiciary, the Constitution provided that judges were to hold their offices "during good behavior" (that is, for life, as a rule); that their salaries could not be diminished during their terms of office; and that they could be removed only by impeachment.

The importance of this independence was underscored by others besides those who wrote the Constitution. . . .

The wisdom of the drafters of the Constitution has been demonstrated by nearly 200 years of history. The resistance to Franklin Roosevelt's effort to "pack the Court" is perhaps the best example.

With only a few examples of judicial misconduct and incompetence, the purifiers are ready to move on the judicial system. Their attack is two-pronged. One focus is on the process of appointment. This process is to be removed from politics, or at least from politicians. While it has been around for a long time, this idea was given new vitality by President Jimmy Carter, who in his campaign promised to appoint judges on the basis of merit, not of politics. His proposal, a little vague around the edges, was to have citizens' commissions instead of Senators recommend judicial appointees. Just how the citizens' commissions were to be set up without politicians' being involved, Carter did not specify. Nor did he explain how the constitutional power of the Senate to confirm judges was to be isolated from any possible advance influence on the choice of nominees.

The Carter proposal might work in a Platonic society, with

"guardians" trained (as Plato suggested) to be protectors of the State. In our society, guardians would undoubtedly be a part of the civil service.

Even the intervention of bar associations in nominations to the federal judiciary, a practice encouraged by some Senators, is questionable. Few Senators, in the course of a six-year term, are called upon to recommend more than one or two nominees for federal courts. If a Senator does not know his constituency, and the lawyers and judges in it, well enough to pick one or two persons every six years, he should resign.

The second prong of the attack on the judiciary consists of proposals to make it easier to remove judges once they have been appointed. Last year the Senate passed a bill establishing the inevitable detached, nonpolitical or apolitical "commission" and a special disciplinary court that could investigate, censure, and remove judges for misconduct, intemperance, or anything deemed "prejudicial to the administration of justice. . . ."

There may well be a reenactment in our society of the state of affairs described by the Duke in *Measure for Measure*: "There is scarce truth enough alive to make societies secure; but security enough to make fellowships accursed."

CRISIS, CRISIS,

WHO'S GOT THE CRISIS?

(*Culpeper News*, APRIL 9, 1981)

The normal conduct of the affairs of state has been made secondary, if not incidental, to what has been labeled "crisis management" by a member of the Kennedy administration. Richard Nixon divided his political life into crises, as reported in his book, *Six Crises* (Watergate by most standards would qualify as number seven). Spokesmen for the Carter administration said that Jimmy Carter had been tested and not found wanting in the "crucible of crisis." An unkind commentator expressed the judgment that the question about President Carter was not whether he would panic in a crisis, but whether he did not in fact panic when there was no crisis.

The crisis mentality is encouraged by television news, especially the evening news, which usually labels about one out of every four news stories as a crisis: real, incipient, lingering, fading, and occasionally dormant.

The first press-identified crisis in the Reagan administration was not one of foreign affairs or of domestic programs or events. It was a crisis provoked by disagreement over who would be in charge of a crisis, if and when one does occur.

The president has said that he was putting Vice President Bush in charge of crises. A number of recent presidents have spoken of giving their vice presidents new responsibilities. Some have, but none has put a vice president in charge of crises. Eisenhower used his secretary of state. Kennedy, by inside report, used McGeorge Bundy. President Johnson relied on Walt Rostow, Nixon on Henry Kissinger, President Ford, according to Joseph Kraft, on someone named Brent Scowcroft, and President Carter was prepared to use Zbigniew Brzezinski in an emergency. The general record of these crisis managers and advisors is such that it might be a good risk to use a vice president or bring back Brent Skowcroft.

Secretary of State Alexander Haig was unhappy over the assignment of crisis direction to Mr. Bush. He seemed to be of the opinion that whoever creates a crisis (the secretary of state being the most likely to do so), should manage the crisis. Haig is also credited with managing, in its latter stages, the Seventh Crisis of the Nixon career. He believed that he handled it well, or as well as could have been done. He may be right.

White House watchers say that this conflict came too early in the life of the administration. They do not say what would have been a good time for it to come. And Joseph Kraft, in a column in the March 29, 1981 *Washington Post*, sets the stage for judgment by saying that "crisis management falls with special force within that ambit of presidential primacy."

If Kraft is right, then any assignment of crisis management responsibility, either before or during a crisis, would seem — unless the assigned manager has special competence and strong public confidence — to show presidential inadequacy.

In my judgment, a much more serious question than the one involving crisis management is that of the relationship between the president and Secretary of State Haig. Two months after the start of this administration, the foreign policy experts have been asking whether or not the president is his own secretary of state. This question has not been raised relative to the president and Secretary Haig. Almost from the moment he was sworn in, Mr. Haig has been acting as though he thought the secretary of state was his own president, a new and somewhat startling conception of the office.

The president might have anticipated trouble, had he been carefully attentive to Mr. Haig's language when Haig first described his conception of the office of secretary of state before congressional committees. He said that he considered himself to be the "vicar" of the president, not the agent, or the humble servant, or the assistant.

The *New York Times* on March 26 reports that a White House aide says Haig has threatened to resign eight times since January 20, 1981. That would be one threat a week for eight weeks. On the principle that a secretary of state, like a cat, has nine lives, Haig has one resignation to go.

WHO'S MINDING THE
AGENDA?

(1988)

For want of an agenda, an administration may be lost.

Vice President Mondale, in explaining the failure of the Carter administration, noted that President Carter was especially handicapped because he had "no agenda" to lean on after he was elected. The difficulties of that administration were further complicated, according to the former vice president, because the White House was also without a mandate.

Currently the lack of an agenda or of control of an agenda, if there is one, seems to be of more concern to politicians, political observers, and analysts than the absence or presence of a mandate.

Soon after the November 1986 elections, the matter of what the National Agenda might be, and who had it, or had one, arose. A *New York Times* article by Steven Roberts quotes Senator John Heinz, a Republican from Pennsylvania, as observing that he didn't sense among the Democrats "much consensus of their agenda for governing the country." How one measures "much consensus," the Senator did not say. Roberts, in the same article, quotes Senator Robert Byrd of West Virginia as saying that as minority leader he had little power to set the agenda.

Closing the "agenda gap," the *Times* notes, is one of the challenges to the Democratic leadership in Congress in 1987. The press generally believed (this was before the Iran-Nicaragua case became public) that although the Democrats would control both the House and the Senate in the 100th Congress, President Reagan still controlled the agenda.

Then along came Representative James Wright of Texas, the Democratic choice to succeed Tip O'Neill as Speaker of the House of Representatives. Wright, the *Washington Post* reports, has asserted "style" and "agenda." How one "asserts an agenda" remains a little vague in the *Post* article. Wright's asserted "agenda" was almost immediately rejected by other Democratic leaders of the House of Representatives.

Meanwhile, there is agenda trouble at other levels of government. The *New York Times* in a headline asks the critical question, "Has Scandal Derailed Koch's Agenda?" The mayor insisted that the agenda had not been derailed, but it had been delayed.

Agenda gaps, and lack of agendas, are not distinctively and solely American. They occur, if a gap or lack of an agenda can be said to occur, in foreign cultures as well as here in the United States — in China, for example. *Washington Post* foreign correspondent Daniel Southerland said that Chinese student protesters do have at least a short-range agenda, but the *Post* headline says that a long-term agenda is lacking.

The problem did not go unnoticed by the Christmas specialty trade; Camalier and Buckley of Washington, D.C. — one of the better leather-goods retail stores in the country — offered among its pre-Christmas goods a leather-covered "agenda" with a clip. The agenda, crafted by the German firm of Gold-Pfeil and offered before Christmas at $100, may now be on sale at reduced prices.

A NOTE ON
THE NEW EQUALITY

(*Commentary*, NOVEMBER 1977)

Dorothy Sayers, in her book *The Mind of the Maker*, quotes a memorable passage from a lecture by L.P. Jacks, given in the 1920s:

> I am informed by philologists that the rise to power of these two words, "problem" and "solution," as the dominating terms of public debate is an affair of the last two centuries, and especially of the 19th, having synchronized, so they say, with a parallel rise to power of the word "happiness. . . ." On the whole, the influence of these words is malign, and becomes increasingly so. They have deluded poor men with Messianic expectations, which are fatal to steadfast

persistence in good workmanship and to well-doing in general. Let the valiant citizen never be ashamed to confess that he has "no solution to the social problem" to offer his fellow-men. Let him offer them rather the service of his skill, his vigilance, his fortitude, and his probity. For the matter in question is not primarily a problem, nor the answer to it a solution.

The words *problem* and *solution* still beset public debate and inquiry. Task forces to identify and define problems are the mark of government at every level, and also of business and institutions and organizations. "Problem-solving" is a national preoccupation. But if problem-solving is still associated with "happiness," it has also come to be associated with a word of comparable, if not greater, significance and influence in social, political, and economic thought today. That word, of course, is *equality*.

Alexis de Tocqueville, in *Democracy in America*, wrote of the powerful appeal and danger of the idea of equality in a democratic society. He wrote also of its potential for demagoguery. I would be less concerned about the rise to popularity of the word, and the idea, if I thought it the result of conscious intention to elicit political support — that is, if those who made the appeal knew that they were being demagogic. I fear, however, that the use of the word is not intentionally demagogic. It seems to approach the automatic "It is good" justification that George Orwell described as characterizing the world order of 1984.

In his inaugural address, President Jimmy Carter said, "We have already found a high degree of personal liberty, and we are now struggling to enhance equality of opportunity." One may well question the president's language. Liberty was a goal of the American Revolution. We have it in this country not because we "found" it but rather as a result of our having declared it a political and social goal and then having achieved it in some measure. As to the president's second point, that "we are now struggling to enhance equality of opportunity," such language does not clearly describe the concept of "equality" as it is applied today. Economic, educa-

tional, political, and cultural equality — and not equality of opportunity, "enhanced" or otherwise — is the goal in the new application.

Economic equality is in this new conception to be achieved primarily through equalizing income. Equalization of wealth — that
is, of wealth already accumulated — may come later. Economic
equality is not conceived as a base upon which differences may
then build, but as an average. One state governor occasionally asks
if it might be better if people doing unpleasant work were paid as
much as or more than those whose work is culturally and physically preferable.

Political economists have developed the notion of a negative income tax as the basis for tax reform. Essentially the idea is this:
Everyone should have enough income to pay taxes at the beginning
or threshold rate, and if one does not have enough income to reach
that level, something should be done to make up for the deficiency.
Where the idea came from, or how the taxable level of income was
chosen as the absolute standard for relative judgments and adjustments, is not clear. It seems that the tax base is to be accepted as
a first principle upon which we are to build. It is an axiom, rather
like "I think, therefore I am." One could as well arbitrarily assert
that everyone should, for the good of the commonwealth, pay $100
in income taxes, and then proceed through measures of redistribution to raise all incomes to the level at which everyone would have
to pay $100 in taxes.

The idea of a negative income tax is appealing. Professors of political economics can diagram its operation. Ideas that can be dia-
grammed, especially in economics and in political science, are very
popular. It is easier to teach with a diagram or chart. A diagram
conveys an impression of certainty. Thus, the business-cycle theory of economics was popular because the charting of the cycle
gave the appearance of scientific order in a confused discipline.
Prosperity was followed by recession, and that in turn by depression, after which the cycle swung up through recovery back to
prosperity. The theory seemed to have the certainty of the seasons

or of the phases of the moon — until the economic moon went down in 1929 and did not come up.

The second area in which the new concept of equality is being applied is in politics and government. The principle of "one person, one vote" was formally recognized in a Supreme Court ruling affecting defined political jurisdictions. The Court did not in its ruling extend the principle to relationships among jurisdictions. The ruling simply said that, within given units of government, each vote should be equal to every other vote. Thus, since the Constitution provides for direct election of the House of Representatives on the basis of population, the rule requires that each congressional district have roughly the same number of persons.

The Constitution also provides that each state, no matter what its size, shall have two Senators. Thus, the citizen of a small state gets proportionally more of a vote in the Senate than the resident of a large state. The Constitution further provides that the president shall be elected through the Electoral College, on a state-by-state basis, thus weighing the votes of smaller states favorably as against those cast in larger states. The drive now is to eliminate that weighting by abolishing the Electoral College and instituting direct popular election of the president. No proposal has yet been made to reduce senatorial representation to a strict population base.

The principle of equality is also applied through the Federal Election Campaign Act, which attempts to equalize the nonvoting influence of citizens on candidates for political office. The present law limits the size of contributions to a political candidate in any one campaign to $1,000 per contributor. This is considered a transitional phase to a time when all campaigns will be publicly financed. The argument for the limitation is that the larger the contribution, the greater the influence a contributor has on the officeholder and the more time he gets to spend with the officeholder. Theoretically, with public financing, every taxpayer will have made an equal contribution and will be entitled to as much time with the officeholder as any other taxpayer. What time nontaxpayers will get has not yet been determined by the reformers. Despite the $1,000 limit on contributions in the last national elections, and the fact that the presidential campaigns were financed principally through federal grants, within a few days of the elections, President-elect Jimmy Carter flew to St. Simons Island (the domain of the Reynolds family) and President Gerald Ford went to Palm Springs — presumably to speak to the average citizens who dwell in those precincts.

It does not take much imagination to foresee a time when citizens might go to court, charging that they were discriminated against because their calls were not taken in presidential telethons and transmitted to the president for his attention. A full practical application of this principle would argue for an equal right to speak or otherwise communicate with all officeholders, even removing the personal screening of Walter Cronkite.

The objective of equalizing communications and influence on officeholders is also sought in efforts to control lobbyists. Proposals generally recommend more thorough regulation of lobbyists, limits on their expenditures, and public disclosure not only of expenditures but also of meetings and communications with officeholders.

It will not be surprising if someone suggests having lobbyists provided at government expense, so as to insulate officeholders from the undue influence of their principles, in somewhat the same way that officeholders are to be insulated from their constituencies. Under this arrangement, anyone who had a case to make to the government would apply for a lobbyist, who would be assigned from a pool in the way that public defenders are assigned by the courts. There could be classes of lobbyists (number one, number two, and so on) who would be assigned by a commission according to the seriousness or difficulty of the case to be made to the government. This procedure would establish a second level of purity and of detachment. A third and a fourth level might be added in pursuit of that absolute certainty and safety sought by the animal in Franz Kafka's story "The Burrow."

The new concept of equality is also applied in government and government-influenced employment practices, in what has been labeled the "quota system." The rationale of the quota system is that, since not every person can be hired, we should have within each employed group a representation or sampling of the total employable work force. Selection currently is on the basis of physiological characteristics of age, sex, and race. There are some obvious historical reasons as to why these standards are being tried. There are also some obvious difficulties in their application, especially if one attempts to extend the principle — as will surely be done — to other racial and ethnic groups, or to groups less easily defined in terms of psychological and cultural differences.

A similar drive to realize the new idea of equality has marked educational development in recent years. The standardized curriculum, quota admissions, open admissions, and free college education are all manifestations of this drive. Full application of the principle could lead to compulsory college education, with the level of education so reduced that all who enter do so with the assurance of successful graduation. With no possible abandonment of hope at any point, they could look forward to something like the judgment of the Dodo after the caucus race in *Alice in Wonderland:* "Everyone has won, and all must have prizes."

What are the dangers in this drive to a newly conceived equality? I see a danger first in the inevitable weakening of those institutions that are expected to give form and direction to society, such as professional and educational institutions, and that have traditionally been treated as having an identity separate from politically controlled areas of society.

I see it also as significantly affecting the individual's conception of his place in society. Most persons cannot stand either physical or cultural isolation, and will seek a base of some certainty in a community of persons and in a cultural complex. The cultural security of Americans traditionally has been found in a society of some tension, but a society in which a balance could be achieved between individual freedom and liberty on the one side and the social good on the other. The alternative now offered, the security of equalization, is depersonalizing. It is a deceptively angelistic conception of man in society. It is one that cannot be sustained. It will in all likelihood move persons in search of security, if not identity, to accept greater and greater socialization in politics, in economics, and in culture.

RELIGION AND POLITICS

(1988)

God is not generally mocked in America, but is more likely to be ignored—except to be blamed for failure. Thus the great "brown-out" in New York City several years ago was called an "act of God" by Con Edison. In the same spirit, the flooding of a subway tunnel in Washington was explained not as a direct act of God, but as one in which God was an accessory before the act. The explanation in this case was, by implication, that on the third day of creation, when the waters were separated from the dry land, God had not anticipated the building of the subway and had not had the foresight to provide a different geological formation in the Potomac River basin.

In presidential campaign years, all is changed. God is recognized, called to witness, asked for help and guidance, given credit for past triumphs of the candidates. Religion, or some aspect of it, is almost certain to become a campaign issue.

There will be nothing like the so-called "Catholic issue" of John Kennedy's campaign of 1960, which moved him to declare to a group of Protestant ministers in Houston that he would make his decisions in the national interest and without regard to "outside religious pressure or dictates. . . ."

Not one of the candidates will have to explain, as did Richard Nixon, that despite the fact that Quakers were pacifists, he was a militant Quaker.

No one will have to explain, as did Senator Charles Percy, a short-time candidate for the presidency, that even though he was a Christian Scientist, he could support medical programs for the people of the nation.

In the Eisenhower campaign of 1952, religion was emphasized more than in any campaign of this century, possibly in the entire history of the country, with the possible exception of the second Lincoln campaign—if Lincoln's second inaugural address reflected the campaign emphasis. In that address, according to one study, there were fourteen references to God, four quotations from Genesis, the Psalms, and Matthew, and numerous allusions to scriptural teachings.

The Eisenhower campaign was presented under the banner of a "crusade," although the cross was vague. A late entry, called "God's float," led the inaugural parade. Religion and government sustained each other during the Eisenhower administration. President Eisenhower urged Americans to spend the first Fourth of July of his administration as a day of penance and prayer. He, on that day, according to columnist Elmer Davis, "caught four fish in the morning, played eighteen holes of golf in the afternoon, and spent the evening playing bridge."

By statute, during that administration, the pledge of allegiance to the flag was changed to include the words *under God*. Legislation prescribing that all U.S. money carry the inscription "In God We Trust" was offered, an action interpreted as a sign of lack of confidence in the secretary of the treasury, George Humphrey. A red, white, and blue postage stamp was issued, bearing the motto "In God We Trust"—this at a time when postal service was becoming slower and less reliable.

There was even some sharing of power between the president and God, according to the president's prayer before sleep (as reported by his wife), in which President Eisenhower asked God to look after the country (and possibly the world) until the president awoke—a kind of night-shift presidency.

The three leading candidates of 1980 were, by their own testimony, born-again Christians. Differences among them, consequently, could not be substantive, but merely relative and of degree. There are no objective standards, either historical or theological, for determining when rebirth occurs, and what results from it. The only sure witness is the person who experiences the rebirth.

Ronald Reagan's rebirth seems to have been a modest one— nothing like that of St. Paul on the road to Damascus. It appears to have been progressive, not marked by startling experiences or a sudden conversion, and stopping at a relatively modest level of religious intensity.

Jimmy Carter was much more specific about his rebirth, possibly because it occurred more recently. He recalled time, place, and consequences. He reported, before he was elected, that he prayed twenty-nine times a day. Later, as president, he was not quite as specific about the number of times he prayed daily, but he said that on days when he felt a "trepidation," he did pray. He did say that he prayed more than anyone else over certain national problems, an assertion hard to prove and hard to dispute, unless the FBI or the CIA knows more than anyone has even suspected.

John Anderson, by his own report, had been reborn. It occurred when he was quite young, about ten or eleven years old, in what he described as a "catastrophic experience" following his exposure to the gospel story of the beheading of John the Baptist.

Anderson's religio-political commitment reached a high point when in the sixties he introduced for the last time a congressional proposal for an amendment to the Constitution that would declare the United States to be a Christian nation. He later said that the proposal was a mistake.

The dropoff from this high point continued in the campaign. In its early stages, Congressman Anderson said that God was his campaign manager or director. He later enlisted the services of public relations expert David Garth.

In the 1984 campaign, President Reagan presented himself as the defender of religion, if not of "the faith." Geraldine Ferraro said that President Reagan was not a good Christian. Other Democrats noted that the president was not a regular attendee at church (as was Richard Nixon, for example).

The Reverend Jesse Jackson, who conducted much of his 1984 primary campaign in churches, accused President Reagan of using religion for political purposes. Walter Mondale regularly pointed out that he was a "minister's kid" and that he prays. Reagan said that the secularists had gone over the wall of separation of church and state by attacking religion. Walter Mondale indicated his belief that Reagan was undermining the wall, or knocking bricks off the top, so as to facilitate a religious invasion of the secular order, and he said that God is not a Republican.

Religion has not figured very strongly in the 1988 presidential campaign, even though two of the candidates, Pat Robertson and Jesse Jackson, are ministers. Jesse Jackson has done some campaigning in churches, but his message has been essentially political. Pat Robertson announced that at least for the duration of his campaign, his relations with the Deity, the more personal ones, would be put on hold. The other candidates generally profess a commitment to the civil religion of America.

There are two safe positions for politicians to take on religion as it bears on politics: the Eisenhower one (Reagan is close to it), described by William Miller in *Piety Along the Potomac* as a "vague religion, strongly held to, and vigorously applied"; or the opposite, safe approach, which is to have, or to say one has, "a strong religion, vaguely held to, and not applied"—which is close to the position taken by some of the candidates this year.

RELIGION, POLITICS, AND ABORTION

(Social Thought, FALL 1986)

Whereas moral disputes are much more common at the level of local and state politics, they emerge at times as issues in national politics. The prime historical example of this was the matter of Prohibition, which was adopted as a constitutional amendment and then repealed seventeen years later. The campaign of 1988 will be marked, it appears, by at least one religion-related issue—that of abortion—whether or not there is a Catholic candidate.

The debate and discussion of that issue, as well as theories of religion-politics relationships, are shaping up much the same as they did before and during John Kennedy's campaign in 1960, al-

The pro-abortionists can find little support or comfort in ancient texts. They can point out that few if any of those who are quoted by the pro-life bloc called abortion murder, and they question the meaning of words in the chosen texts. They can point out that through the centuries philosophers, theologians, and physiologists have disagreed as to when the fetus becomes viable (with that term also in need of further definition). Some, in medieval times, believed that the male fetus was viable after forty days and the female after ninety days, while others held that the variance was between forty days for males and eighty days for females. In a later century, there was serious argument as to whether the baptism of a fetus in the womb in anticipation of trouble, via tube, was valid, or whether valid baptism could be administered only after the fetus had been exposed to the light of day (or dark of night).

In our time, the efforts to reduce the range of differences between pro-abortion advocates and those opposed to abortion have had little success. The trimestral division that the Supreme Court attempted to draw in the landmark case of *Roe* v. *Wade* has not been accepted or applied with any discernible success—nor has the physiological standard of viability under natural conditions outside the womb.

The case against arbitrary and forceful governmental action is best made by the record, which shows that the practice continues to grow despite condemnation of abortion over the centuries, and despite civil and religious laws condemning it. I have seen no report of decline in the number of abortions during the Reagan administration, which repeatedly affirms its opposition to abortion and has moved affirmatively to cut off government funds for abortions. The attempt to decide the issue at the federal rather than the state level is at least debatable, but the abortion issue is not likely to be left at the state level.

This is no easy time. There is no place of retreat for either moralists or politicians. Moralists must be prepared to suffer the "unhappiness" that is their lot, consistent with what philosopher Jacques Maritain wrote of them and for them: "When moralists insist on the immutability of moral principles they are reproached for imposing unlivable requirements on us. When they explain the way in which these immutable principles are to be put into force, taking into account the diversity of concrete situations, they are reproached for making morality relative. In both cases, however," he added, "they are upholding the claims of reason to direct life. The task of ethics is a humble one, but it is also magnanimous in carrying the mutable application of immutable moral principles, even in the midst of the agony of an unhappy world, as far as there is in it a gleam of humanity."

Beyond, behind, or below the moralists are the politicians, whose task is more modest, more humble, more pragmatic than that of the moralists. They work in the arena of political decision, where, as educator Ernest Lefever observed, "one can be pure or responsible, but not both."

There is little to be gained by attempting to link the issue of abortion with other issues of high moral content, such as nuclear war or poverty, although undoubtedly poverty can be or may be given as justification for abortions. Nor should a politician be allowed the defense, whether for or against abortion, of what he or she determines to be a "consensus." Consensus is at best an ill-defined condition, and one that can dissipate quickly. The time has come to take the rules by which governmental intervention in matters of morality are to be judged, out of the academic rooms and beyond abstract reflection.

First we must ask whether the subject matter of possible action (in this case, abortion) is wrong in itself and a threat to social order and stability, and whether the action proposed is, as St. Thomas Aquinas said, "ordainable to the common good."

It may be conceded that abortion is wrong in itself, although some might dispute that concession, but certainly the second part of the proposition—that it is "a threat to social order and stability" under all conditions—is arguable.

On the other hand, it has not been proved that abortion is good or necessary for the social order or "ordainable to the common good," even though a plausible case may be made for the good of a particular abortion, in the interest of a mother or a family.

Even though the questions under the first rule were answered affirmatively in support of those opposed to abortion, or left somewhat unsettled, as they are, additional standards should be applied. Again, a formulation of St. Thomas is applicable. "Now," he wrote, "human law is framed for the multitude of human beings, the majority of whom are not perfect in virtue. Therefore, human laws do not forbid all vices, from which the virtuous abstain, but only the more grievous vices, from which it is possible for the majority to abstain, and chiefly those that are injurious to others, without the prohibition of which human society could not be maintained."

The application of this rule in contemporary circumstances does not yield results fully justifying rigorous anti-abortion laws and enforcement of them, and also leaves two other difficult questions to be answered.

The first is that of whether government can effectively control a practice as personal and private, and as much a part of the culture as abortion seems to be, without forcing persons seeking abortions to have recourse to illegal services and unqualified practitioners.

A second and final question is that of whether, in acting against abortion absolutely, society would seek to impose a rule of conduct that would require, if conformed to, heroic virtue from those affected.

Heroic virtue is highly subjective and personal, yet there is a rationally determinable range of demands beyond which prudential determination can be made that ordinary virtue is insufficient. The situation requiring more than ordinary virtue may be personal, yet it may be one for which society is responsible. In the latter case, society has the responsibility to undertake the alleviation of the conditions requiring heroic virtue, or, failing that, to be tolerant of those who do not meet the hard test.

For many persons in our country, rejection of abortion may require heroic virtue because of poverty, inadequate housing, disordered community life, disintegration of the family, cultural attitudes, failure of society to provide alternatives to abortion, or personal handicaps (physical, mental, or emotional).

Thus, some conclusions:

> • Those opposed to abortion should continue their moral opposition to abortion but be careful to avoid becoming like the Christians described by Dom Verner Moore—persons standing on shore advising a drowning person to take good, deep breaths of fresh air.
> • Opponents are justified in objecting to the use of public money, including that gathered from their taxes, to propagate and defend abortion or to pay for abortion.
> • Opponents should move strongly against the conditions that justify, or are used to justify, abortion—principally (1) unemployment—which will not be significantly reduced in the United States unless there is a redistribution of existing work; (2) inadequate and improper housing—a problem that needs a massive response, one comparable to what went into the nation's highway building program in the fifties; (3) family disintegration—the integrity of the family must be reestablished and stabilized. The community, government, or private individuals should help, if necessary, with a national, federally financed program of support for the poor, especially for poor children; child-care centers, nursery schools, adoption programs, and an expansion of the foster home programs; and assistance during and after pregnancy for those who might otherwise have abortions.

The magnitude, seriousness, and complexity of the problem of abortion requires a response of equal magnitude, sustained by personal and community commitment. It is anticipated that success will be limited and slow in coming, and that the sustaining force may be hope, supported by the minimal optimism expressed by Thomas More in *Utopia:* "If evil opinion and naughty persuasion cannot be utterly and altogether plucked out . . . if you cannot, even as you would, remedy vices which habit and custom have confirmed, yet this is no cause for leaving and forsaking the commonwealth."

A FITTING MEMORIAL
TO THOSE WHO FOUGHT
AND DIED IN VIETNAM

(Rappahannock News, DECEMBER 2, 1982)

"Too long a sacrifice can make a stone of the heart." So wrote William Butler Yeats in his poem "Easter 1916," about the Irish rebellion against the British that year in Dublin.

And he followed that line with this question: "O, when may it suffice?"

So too might he have written of the grief, rancor, resentment, disorder, and confusion of "hearts and minds" that have run on in our nation since the ending of the Vietnam War.

Yeats left the final settlement to a tribunal other than a human one and set the measure of human response in the next lines of his poem.

> That is heaven's part, our part
> To murmur name upon name,
> As a mother names her child
> When sleep at last has come
> On limbs that had run wild.

The monument to the dead of the Vietnam War is a material representation of Yeats's words, as was the reading of the names of all the dead in the ceremony at the National Cathedral.

What better memorial for a war than simply to list the names, carved in stone, without rank or distinction, and to have each of those names spoken, at least once. It was a lonely war for those who fought it. Heroism was a part of every day's mission, not of heroic landings or assaults. There was no stage in this war for officers, in battle jackets of their own design, standing on high cliffs and looking into the distance or making landings after the cameramen had been sent ashore.

The designer of the memorial, those who approved it, those who carved the names and set the stones—all are to be commended. Like the war, the memorial has no clear beginning or ending. In one perspective, it rises from the earth; in another, it gradually descends. Only the marking of the years of the deaths sets any order. One veteran in attendance at the memorial service is reported to have said, "It's just like the war; it's not complete. Where's the statues they're going to add?" He was half right. The memorial was like the war, as he said, but it was also complete, although he thought not. There should be no statues. Maya Lin, the designer, with her Oriental background, may understand, better than we do, continuity—without clear beginnings and endings. She may also have understood clearly what she meant to state in her design. She may have been moved, as artists sometimes are, beyond understanding into the range of special inspiration.

Indiana governor Roger D. Branigin, in a moment of truth in 1968,

said that he was against the Vietnam War because it was the first
war the United States had had that was not a "happy war."

The war was not only not "happy," but positively unhappy—so
much so that novelists and playwrights only recently have begun
to write of it. In earlier years, only poets dared, or were driven, to
write of it: George Bowering, Robert Bly, Richard Wilbur, Richard
Snyder, Lewis Turco, and many others.

I tried a poem to note and explain this absence:

> Kilroy is gone,
> the word is out,
> absent without leave
> from Vietnam.
>
> Kilroy
> who wrote his name
> in every can
> from Poland to Japan
> and places in between
> like Sheboygan and Racine
> is gone,
> absent without leave
> from Vietnam.
>
> Kilroy
> who kept the dice
> and stole the ice
> out of the BOQ.
>
> Kilroy
> whose name was good
> on every IOU
> in World War II
> and even in Korea
> is gone
> absent without leave
> from Vietnam.

Kilroy
the unknown soldier
who was the first to land
the last to leave,
with his own hand
has taken his good name
from all the walls
and toilet stalls.

Kilroy
whose name around the world
was like the flag unfurled
has run it down
and left Saigon
and the Mekong
without a hero or a song
and gone
absent without leave
from Vietnam.

More profound than all of these poetic reflections was the note accompanying a Bronze Star medal, given to me anonymously in 1968 (I give it with misspellings):

> I received a medal for vallor in Vietnam. But vallor is a corollary of morality and this war is not moral. It has corrupted the men who fight it. It has divided the nation which conceived it.
>
> I cannot begin to recount the number of distasteful tasks, I witnessed American soldiers perform, including the beating of women and children and the corruption of an entire population.
>
> Therefore I cannot in clear conscience retain this reward for actions which in essence served to supress the freedom of the Vietnamese people.

Yeats may well have given the best explanation in answer to his own question about deaths in 1916 ("Was it needless death after all?"), when he wrote:

> . . . For all that is done and said.
> We know their dream; enough
> To know they dreamed and are dead;
> And what if excess of love
> Bewildered them till they died?

CONSEQUENCES OF
THE VIETNAM WAR
AND GOVERNMENT POLICIES
OF THE SEVENTIES

The Vietnam War had a disordering, disrupting, and even corrupting effect in major areas of government and politics. It corrupted the military establishment. Officers and spokesmen for the military not only made major misjudgments about the war but also misrepresented, even falsified, reports of what was happening in the war.

The military were further corrupted by the use of methods of warfare contrary to American tradition and the code of military conduct: firing on undefended villagers, making little or no distinction between combatants and noncombatants, using napalm and defoliants, resorting to executions. My Lai was the prime example.

Officers allowed themselves to be used to sustain the political case for the war. General William Westmoreland, a notable example, returned to defend the war before the Congress.

The war corrupted the administration, the presidency, the CIA, the Senate, the House of Representatives, and other institutions of government. It corrupted the press, the media, and the language, going well beyond Orwellian language, until finally progress or lack of progress was reported in numbers, such as body counts and kill ratios.

It corrupted the Democratic party, its procedures and its substantive stand on the war in Vietnam.

It prepared the way for the fiscal disorder to follow, a disorder that was manifest in the inflation of the Carter administration and is reflected in the massive debt (federal) largely accumulated during the Reagan administration.

While too little attention was given to substantive disorders, too much attention was directed to procedural change, as the answer to most long-recognized and troubling problems of government and society.

Evidently encouraged by a budget surplus of $3.2 billion in 1969, and a deficit of only $2.8 billion in 1971, Congress and the Nixon administration approved revenue sharing, something the states accepted quickly. Let the federal government (which some economists, projecting a growing economy and the end of the war, said would be hard pressed to spend all of its collected taxes) distribute money to the states. The slogan for states operating on monies received from the federal government could well have been "Representation without Taxation." (Two governors exhibited fiscal responsibility in using those distributed federal funds: Carter and Reagan.) The federal government began to run short of money; the war did not end in 1970 and the growth of the economy slowed.

When the federal debt continued to grow, Congress did not choose to cut appropriations or raise more money as a solution but passed a resolution on budget control. The budget process, it was held, would bring the budget under control. Obviously, it did not. Budget deficits have been greater since the passage of the 1974 budget resolution than they were at any time in the earlier history of the country.

With the budget out of control, and inflation rates growing, Congress took another step toward automatic government. It indexed government salaries, including those of members of Congress, and indexed federal pensions and Social Security payments, without providing an adequately indexed base to support the inflation-moved increases.

Then, in the latter half of the decade, having come close to losing control of the economy through budget and fiscal reforms, Congress and the reformers turned to politics and to governmental procedures as the way to salvation.

In 1975–76 the new provisions of the Federal Election Campaign Law were passed. The theory was that if the government paid for political actions, corruption would be reduced if not eliminated, and better persons would be elected to national offices. The financing, currently in effect, applies only to presidential races. Two presidents have been elected since passage of the law, Jimmy Carter and Ronald Reagan.

To improve its operation, Congress was reorganized. The principal target of reorganization was the seniority system, a system that, if it did nothing else, accomplished what Gilbert Chesterton said was accomplished by having the eldest son, or daughter, of a monarch follow his or her parent to the throne—"It saved a lot of trouble."

And then, from 1977 to 1979, with starts and stops, progress and retreat, the House and the Senate each adopted codes of ethics. Since the codes were adopted, but not necessarily because of their application or enforcement, public disclosure of moral failings on the part of members of Congress has demonstrated that the adoption of codes did not either ensure the election of "good men" or or keep those in office on the straight and narrow.

In addition, and of quasi-substantive significance, was the War Powers Act, a kind of after-the-act defense by those who did not oppose the Vietnam War when it was in progress.

The decade of the eighties got off to a reasonably bad start. Taxes, the one immediate response to inflation and to its control, were indexed. There was pressure to extend federal funding of campaigns beyond presidential elections, where it has not worked well, to include congressional elections, where it is likely to work even less well, and support for constitutional amendments to balance the budget.

The whole reform record sustains Gilbert Chesterton's judgment cited earlier, that "the Puritans wind up killing St. George and keeping the dragon."

VIETNAM:

DID IT REALLY HAPPEN?

(1987)

In 1967, when it was becoming evident that the war in Vietnam was going badly, Senator George Aiken of Vermont suggested that the best way to end the war was for President Lyndon Johnson to declare that we had won the war, bring the troops home, and hold a great victory celebration. The Senator's suggestion was looked upon by some, especially in the Johnson administration, as frivolous. In the years following, as the war went from bad to worse, the wisdom of the Senator's recommendation became clearer and clearer.

As more and more reports are made public, and as persons who were involved in the war break silence, it begins to appear that one of the difficulties in its conduct was that no one was either in charge or responsible.

A 1983 CBS special report sought to discover why the numbers of Vietcong and North Vietnamese military personnel were consistently reported to the public at about 50 percent of the amount that the CIA estimated to be present—estimates that some officers believed to be true and reported to their superiors. Most of the commanding officers, including General William Westmoreland, the commander of American troops in Vietnam, could not recall having revised or adjusted the estimates, or, if they had participated in revisions, could not remember why they had reduced the enemy's numbers or why the revision nearly always was about half of the CIA estimates.

The *New York Times*, too, carried another report of no-recall, forgetfulness, and loss of memory among those in high places. In this case, the "cannot recall" syndrome affected both civilians and military personnel. At issue was a report by the Air Force on the spraying of herbicides and defoliants on Laos and Vietnam during the war. The report, covering the years from 1961 to 1971, was made public under the Freedom of Information Act, as a result of a lawsuit by the Veterans Task Force on Agent Orange. The spraying, according to the report, was initiated in Vietnam at the request of President Ngo Dinh Diem, and extended into Laos in late 1965.

General Westmoreland said he could not remember ordering spraying in Laos but added, "It could have been done by people in my headquarters without my being involved."

The report states that in 1961, Secretary of Defense Robert McNamara "continued to hold open the option of disguising the defoliation program as a South Vietnamese operation." The secretary had, and has, a reputation for not forgetting anything. (Once, in answer to a question from Senator Wayne Morse about how many tanks there were in Latin America, he replied, without consulting a note or an aide, that there were 974 tanks; and then he added the clinching information that that number was 60-percent as many tanks as there were in Bulgaria.) In responding to questions about the defoliation project, he said that he was "unable to recall the details of defoliation, or who ordered or approved" it.

The report also states that Secretary of Defense McNamara and Secretary of State Dean Rusk directed that in response to any press queries, the dropping of herbicides on Laos should be reported as reconnaissance flights made at the request of "Laotian authorities." Both Mr. Rusk and Mr. McNamara, according to the *Times*, said that they do not have any recollection of that directive.

The lesser officials Frederick Nolting and Roswell Gilpatric, in the government during these years, both said that they could not remember recommendations and presentations attributed to them in the Air Force report. Maybe Vietnam didn't happen.

INDUSTRIES AND JOBS

OF THE FUTURE

(1988)

Chronic underemployment and unemployment are the mark of the American economy. With approximately 7 million persons currently listed as unemployed, liberal and Democratic economists and politicians are rerunning both their old lines and some left behind by George Meany. "The government is the employer of last resort." "The housing industry must be stimulated." "Retrain more people." "Restore the Civilian Conservation Corps." "Pass another Full Employment Act." "Restrict imports."

Conservatives, speaking largely through the Reagan administration, recite their litany. "More capital investment." "Fewer government controls." "Let every employer hire one unemployed person." "Supply-side economics." "More unemployment."

It is suggested that American workers need to become more productive to compete effectively in world markets and thereby create more jobs.

The policies, both liberal and conservative, that have been pursued over the last forty years have not accomplished their objectives. Instead, they have led to national economic instability.

The "normal" current unemployment rate has more than doubled in forty years. It hits hardest at the young—those actively seeking work and those whose education and stability are affected by their parents' unemployment. It perpetuates the bondage of an underclass of ill-educated, ill-housed, ill-nourished, and ill-cared-for people whose potential contribution to national prosperity is thrown away. And it sows the seeds of future social and political instability.

The need to face the problem of unemployment in other than piecemeal fashion is therefore threefold: It is moral, political, and economic. We regularly urge the redistribution of land in developing nations, but we shy away from proposals to redistribute work in the United States. Jobs are the basic property in industrialized societies, and it is proper to suggest they be shared if the United States is to advance beyond permanent high unemployment.

Shortening working hours has economic, moral, and social justification. Shortened working time would afford more people the dignity of a job, as well as the necessary spiritual refreshment of true leisure time. It would spread income across social barriers, thus leading to lower taxation rates on any one segment of society because all segments would be contributing. And shortening working time, by diminishing unemployment, would relieve the strain on social cohesion that continued economic inequality renders dangerous.

Opposition to this idea is formidable; however, the philosophical case against redistributing work is faulty. The traditional view of work was that work was an assistant to mankind, not a master. In the course of history, however, the Protestant transformation of Christian values gave rise to changes in how work was viewed. These alterations of traditional thought were explored in the early part of this century with some thoroughness by Max Weber, by whom the phrase *Protestant work ethic* became widely distributed. Citing American colonial history, Weber demonstrated the theological method by which work came to take primacy over the person who does the work.

> For six pounds a year you may have the use of one hundred pounds . . . . He that spends a groat a day idly, spends idly above six pounds a year, which is the price for the use of one hundred pounds. He that idly wastes a groat's worth of his time per day, one day with another, wastes the privilege of using one hundred pounds each day. He that idly loses five shillings' worth of time, loses five shillings, and might as prudently throw five shillings into the sea. He that loses five shillings, not only loses that sum, but all the advantage that might be made by turning it in dealing, which by the time that a young man becomes old, will amount to a considerable sum of money.

Our society is morally dominated by the work ethic. We measure human progress by investments that increase the annual sales of fast foods, fast horses, and fast bombers.

Jacques Ellul, a contemporary French philosopher, makes the point that the biblical text most often cited to prove that work is part of human nature actually includes none of the known attributes of work. In Genesis 2, Adam is told to "cultivate" and to "guard" Eden. Yet "this original notion includes none of the characteristics of work! True, cultivation is required, but it has little utility, because the Garden already flourishes on its own without any particular human help."

In his discussion of the condition of work in the Roman Empire, Jacques Ellul is equally incisive.

> In the most general terms, the ideal human life involved the total absence of work. Work was not invested with any moral value. On

160

the contrary, it was the mark of an inferior condition, of degradation (in that it was negation of liberty, being of the order of necessity!). The ideal of the free Roman, not just of the patrician, or the rich, but of all citizens, was leisure—not laziness or rest, but a certain conception of life.

In considering the place of work in life and society, Ellul notes that in former times work played a role different from the one it does at present, when it serves to define, and even to give value to, most people's lives.

> Slaves in antiquity had nothing in common with the blacks of the West Indies in the 17th and 18th centuries, whose condition was atrocious. By contrast, Greek and Roman slaves were not weighted down with work. Their chores were generally light, and they had a great deal of leisure time. Slavery was more a condition of the deprivation of liberty or citizenship than of work.

By the Middle Ages, ancient forms of slavery had been replaced by serfdom, but restrictions on overworking one's dependents applied as strongly as did the rest of the moral code. The philosophy of salvation by work alone runs contrary to the history of Western philosophy and theology. The historical case against redistributing work is generally misstated. The rise in Western prosperity since the Renaissance is not a function of people working more hours, but of more people working and more capital investment.

The commercial, economic, and social case against shortened working hours is the least convincing, in that it is essentially shortsighted and primarily greed-motivated. Corporations fear that hiring more workers, while lowering the working hours but not the compensation of existing workers, will raise their expenses without a concomitant rise in productivity and profits.

There are no surprises in the argument. Negative statements prevalent in the Middle Ages, the Industrial Revolution, and the Depression are recycled. Laziness, drunkenness, and similar proclivities to waste were assigned then, and are assigned now, as being the most probable outcomes of higher incomes and less unemployment for workers.

Henry Ford knew better. His concept of overpaying (by 1914 standards) his workers, and of limiting their working hours to the then-radical figure of eight hours per day and five days per week, was not rooted in any wild beneficence. Ford noted that he couldn't sell many of his automobiles to his workers if they didn't make enough to afford them, and then have some time off to use them.

CORPORATIONS

(*Ethikos*, SEPTEMBER/OCTOBER 1987)

James Kent, in his *Commentaries on American Law*, published early in the nineteenth century, observed that "the number of charters of incorporations" was increasing in the United States with disturbing rapidity. "We are multiplying in this country to an unparalleled extent the institution of corporations," he wrote, "and giving them a flexibility and variety of purpose unknown to the Roman or to the English law."

Kent's warning has gone unheeded, and the drive to incorporation runs beyond the point he feared.

In America today, the corporation is not only the principal instrument for conducting business and finance, but also a major instrument for influencing and managing education, religion, communications, sports, and politics.

About 80 percent of the measurable economic activities of the United States are directed through corporate organizations operating under state charters. Corporate power is a growing force in determining United States foreign policy and military policy and strategy. Multinational and international corporations are intimately involved in foreign policy decisions and their execution. This influence is more subtle and integrated than it was years ago. Early in this century, corporations influenced foreign policy, but that influence could usually be identified, and was to a large extent subject to government direction, or at least coincided with government policy. Corporations were to a degree agents of the government, although in some cases, in a kind of reciprocal arrangement, the government became the agent of the corporations.

United Fruit Company, for example, carried on trade and also executed, or sustained, national policy in Central and South America. American sugar companies controlled trade in sugar and strongly influenced national policy toward Central American countries, especially toward Cuba, from the time of the Spanish-American War until the time of Castro. The relationship was noted by Mr. Dooley, in writing of the Spanish-American War, when he observed that he would rather be subject to a Spanish nobleman than to an American vegetable (the sugar beet).

The power of multinational, or supranational, corporations goes beyond that exercised by companies such as United Fruit in earlier times. Multinationals are not agents, but they carry the attributes of sovereign countries. For example, when President Reagan undertook to prevent or discourage Dresser Industries from selling high-technology pipeline equipment through its multinational connection to builders of the gas pipeline from the USSR to Europe, he found that he was without power to intervene directly.

The involvement of private industry in providing material for World War II established a relationship between the military and private suppliers, which in the postwar period became the military-industrial complex. That complex, which had not quite come together at the end of the World War II, and was threatened by defense budget cuts in the years before the Korean War (Truman cut back to less than $20 billion), was in place when the Korean War ended. Defense budgets have continued to climb ever since. The military-industrial complex is protected by (1) the change in name of the War Department to the Department of Defense (wars are limited and historical, defense is forever and unlimited; (2) the establishment of the Air Force, which emerged as the popular, heroic, and romantic service after World War II, and the establishment of the Air Force Academy to sustain its separateness; (3) the substitution of the volunteer (mercenary) army for compulsory military service, and (4) a budget providing nearly $300 billion in annual appropriations.

The corporation has developed into a separate center of power. Its power was not anticipated by or provided for in the Constitution. Its power has not been subject to the general laws dealing with business and financial practices. The corporation has assumed functions that go far beyond its original economic purposes.

Weapons plans conceived by corporate engineering, research, and development departments can become the basis for both military tactics and strategic changes. Weapons systems and strategic projections by the military depend on corporate potential for manufacture.

The influence of corporations on culture and education is growing. Dow Chemical cut off its support of the University of Michigan because of student protests against the use of the napalm it manufactured. In Minnesota, a number of corporations have organized a special committee that meets with governors, archbishops, and heads of universities and colleges, among others, to determine who will receive grants and for what purpose. Corporate heads act much like the nobles of England, sitting down with the king or the archbishop.

We now have a kind of corporate feudalism, one that fits the schoolboy definition of *feudalism* as a system in which everybody belongs to someone and everyone else belongs to the king. In its modern form, nearly every worker belongs to some corporation. Everyone else—in civil service, on welfare, on workers' compensation or Social Security—belongs to the government.

I hesitate to make a direct comparison between today's corporation employees and the serfs of the Middle Ages, yet there are disturbing similarities. Many people become economic captives of the corporations for which they work. Pension programs, family health plans, seniority rewards, vacation, and sick leave all limit the freedom of employees to move to other corporations and other types of work. This is true not only of blue-collar workers but also of executives and professionals. I have talked with newspaper people who say, "I can't quit this newspaper and take another job because I would lose my pension program, or my family medical plan. I'm an indentured servant. I'm caught." An indentured servant may be a few steps above a serf, but that is not much consolation.

The loss of freedom that goes with working for a corporation is not always accompanied by security, something that serfs in the Middle Ages *did* have. Many corporations, particularly those in the military and aerospace industries, stockpiled engineers and other professionals during the boom period of the 1960s. When the corporations faced financial difficulties, or when they no longer needed the professionals, they simply cut them loose to become displaced persons in our society. In recent years, a relief pitcher in the minor leagues has had more security than a Ph.D. in physics working for a major corporation.

Feudal lords had certain obligations toward the poor, something that cannot be said of our corporations. America's poor and minorities, its undereducated and underfed, are not even the serfs of corporate feudalism. They are its outcasts.

The feudal analogy also holds when one considers the relations between the federal government and large corporations. In case after case of confrontation between the two in the last fifteen to twenty years, the issues have been settled by negotiation. When the question of sending an ambassador to the Vatican was raised in 1960, I suggested that there were other centers of power where we were unrepresented and that were far ahead of the Vatican in terms of influence. For example, a president might first send an ambassador to the Pentagon and then to several of the giant corporations: General Motors, Du Pont, General Electric, U.S. Steel, some of the oil companies.

The dealings of the government with the steel industry over the years illustrate the feudal character of the corporation-government relationship even more clearly. During the Korean War, President Harry Truman tried to prevent a steel strike by ordering his secretary of commerce to take over and operate the steel mills. The case was taken to the Supreme Court, which held that the order was unconstitutional. Subsequent challenges to the industry were handled differently. The Kennedy administration responded to a major price increase not by law or by appeal to courts but by public denunciation, the threat of shifting military purchases to steel companies that had not raised their prices, and even some use of the FBI.

The Johnson administration called presidents of steel companies to the White House for "jawboning sessions." The message was that prices should be kept down. It seemed that if the steel executives fixed prices in the White House, it was quite all right, but if they fixed them in Pittsburgh, they might go to jail. It was as though the king had called in the barons and said to them, "If you agree to these prices in my presence, they are sanctioned. But if you do it by yourselves in the provinces, you are in trouble."

Corporate influence on sports is clearly manifest in the Olympics. In 1984, twenty-nine corporations paid at least $4 million each to the Los Angeles Olympic Organizing Committee to become "official game sponsors." The group included United Airlines, Buick Motor Division of General Motors, Anheuser-Busch, and Fuji Photo Film Co. Ltd. But other corporations cut in on the Olympic pie by sponsoring game-related activities. Ford, for example, was the official car for the National Volleyball Association. Miller Beer funded two U.S. Olympic training centers. Eastman Kodak sponsored the U.S. track and field team and other summer and winter Olympic teams. The official corporations used the the logo of the U.S. Olympic Committee; others, who bought advertising television time from ABC-TV, used ABC's logo.

The intrusion of corporate influence, according to Andrew Strenk (identified as the resident historian on the staff of the 1984 Olympic Organizing Committee), introduced a new standard for the selection of events to be included in the Olympics. It is the "bottom line." Strenk has not yet proved himself as an Olympic historian, but he deserves credit for his openness in reporting the new standards upon with Olympic decisions are to be based.

The compelling consideration as to which events will be included in the Olympic Games, and when and how they will be represented, is, according to Strenk, "dollars and business sense. Behind the scenes," he reports, "the Olympic Committee has to ask how many people will watch the sport? Can we sell out the stadium?" One must ask, before all else, "Is it adaptable to television?"

It seems that the old saying "Who pays the piper calls the tune" will again be proven true. Or, as Nelson Rockefeller is reported to have said to Diego Rivera, who objected to making changes in the mural he was painting in Rockefeller Center, "It's my wall."

Just what corporate dominance, through television marketing and application of the "bottom line" rule, will do to the Olympics has not been demonstrated, but there are indications of what is to come when athletes run not for the "finish line" or the "goal," but for the "bottom line." It is not that the Olympics have been pure and free of outside influence. The seeds of commercialism and of professionalism were present at the first meeting of the Greek athletes at Olympia in 776 B.C. Winning athletes were given not only wreaths and trophies, but also free meals and a lifetime exemption from taxation. This latter reward could be a powerful motivation if given to U.S. athletes today.

Three hundred years after the establishment of the Olympic

Games, Euripides—poet, playwright, and athlete—wrote that "out of the tens of thousands of ills in Greece, none is worse than the tribe of professional athletes."

In the modern version of the Olympics, after their revival in 1896, political rather than commercial and economic forces appear to have influenced the games in selection of events, eligibility of participants, choice of referees, equipment, and location.

We have come a long way since the 1896 revival, which was limited principally to classical contests of speed, endurance, and strength of individual athletes. In 1984, sailing, kayaking, board-sailing, and judo were included in the competitions. None of these sports is likely to last long in Olympic meetings, however, unless they provide photo opportunities and receive popular support from television viewers. Otherwise, they are likely to go the way of some of the events that have been included in past games—for example, fishing, the firing of large-caliber cannon, musical composition, and even poetry. On the other hand, contests that have been tried in the past and dropped may be brought back because of their commercial viability—Indian club swinging, one-handed weightlifting, tug-of-war, and holding one's breath under water, an event included only once and won by a Frenchman who stayed submerged in the Seine for sixty-eight seconds.

Woodrow Wilson, writing nearly 100 years after James Kent, admonished people against referring to corporations as not having full social or political or moral responsibility. They are no more than what they are made by law and, in the case of most American corporations, are committed, no matter what the substance of their operations—culture, education, publications, sports, or business and finance—to profit-making, to the bottom line.

REBATES AND PRE-BATES

(Washington Star, AUGUST 7, 1977)

The revival of the rebate as an economic and moral force is a phenomenon of the last few years. Before its restoration, the rebate was more than slightly suspect. It was associated with the robber barons of the 1880s and 1890s and, more intimately, with John D. Rockefeller. He persuaded or forced the railroads that carried his oil shipments to give him rebates on what he had paid them for carrying his oil.

With rebates under a cloud, promoters turned to discounts, trading stamps, an occasional one-cent sale, and nonmonetary deceptions. The rebate was shunned. Then came the automobile sales slump a few years ago, and with it the revival of the rebate—first by Chrysler, the company in most difficulty, and then by Ford and General Motors.

The rebate offered by the automobile companies was no simple, old-fashioned or traditional rebate. It was not given immediately or directly. A car purchaser did not, for example, pay $4,400 for his car to the local dealer and then and there get $400 back. He financed the car at $4,400, paid the local dealer, left with his car, and trusted. The rebate came later and from Detroit. The money was sent away and then it came back.

There was nothing crass or vulgar about the return. No bargaining or haggling. The amount was as promised, but the money was different. It was marked by Detroit through a process rather like the sale of indulgences in late medieval times. The pardoners sold locally, but the indulgences were granted from Rome.

The rebates worked. Automobile sales went up. Since what is good for General Motors is good for the country (the Scripture according to Charlie Wilson, former president of General Motors and former secretary of defense), the idea of using rebates was picked up almost immediately by other businesses. With appliance dealers, the rebate became the "in" thing. Rebates were offered to those who purchased washing machines, power mowers, toasters, and so forth. Discounts were out. Newspapers and magazines followed. They did not make introductory offers at reduced rates; they offered rebates, which were really pre-bates.

The government has learned many of its tricks from the corporate world. For example, corporations had retirement programs for their employees before the Social Security program was adopted. Corporations began providing unemployment compensation before it was provided through the government. Corporate health insurance ran well ahead of any consideration of national health insurance. And Henry Ford established, in his five-dollar-per-day wage, an example for the federal minimum-wage program. So the government was quick to see the virtues of the rebate.

Subsidies had become unpopular. Why not "rebates" instead?

Refunds of taxes carried no special credit, since they suggested mistakes in the first place. Tax cuts were taken for granted or as deserved. But the rebate was something different. Rebating is a positive act, involving a transfer to a person of money over which he had lost control. The money to be rebated had become the government's money. Now that money was to be given back to the taxpayer, not refunded.

In paying taxes for 1975, some taxpayers were permitted to take what was labeled as a 10-percent rebate on their 1974 taxes. Actually it was a reduction of 1975 taxes, roughly equivalent to 10 percent of the taxes paid by the citizen in the previous year.

The Democrats, coming on in 1977, were not limited by the simple Republican rebate concept of 1975. The Carter administration saw almost unlimited possibilities in the rebate. It did not need to be given to everyone who had paid taxes or in the same amount or percentage to all taxpayers. It could be given to some who had not paid taxes at all—an experience that might motivate the beneficiary to greater efforts to earn enough so that he would pay taxes, which achievement in turn would make him eligible for more and larger rebates.

Since the rebate was so popular, why not rebates instead of tax credits or deductions? There were proposals for tax rebates to solve social and economic problems that had resisted subsidies, tax concessions, credits, and deductions, and even affirmative action. There were proposals for rebates to encourage the installation of insulation, of storm windows and doors; to encourage the use of solar energy and wind power; and to induce people to change over to electric cars.

President Carter's proposal for a special postal rate for "citizens' mail" might better be handled through rebates. Handwritten letters could be turned in as proof of claim to a rebate. There could be graduated rebates—say, ten cents on letters to mothers or wives, eight cents to fathers or husbands, five cents to siblings and friends.

The rebate concept has even reached religion, at least in Michigan, where one church sign offered this inducement: "Come to church on Sunday. Get a rebate on eternal life."

I was unable to attend the advertised services, but, on reflection, concluded that a rebate on eternal life must be an updated variant of an indulgence.

LINK THE DOLLAR TO

. . . TO . . . TO . . .

(New York Times, June 20, 1983)

It has been suggested of late in certain quarters of the financial world that the floating dollar, approved by Richard Nixon with an assist from then Secretary of the Treasury John Connally, has not done much for world trade and economic stability, and that a dollar stabilized in a vague relationship to gold or some suitable commodity might do better.

But as a reliable standard, gold suffers from manipulation at the hands of South Africans and Communists. Copper, on the other hand, widely available and less subject to market fluctuations than gold, would be an ideal substitute for gold. In the opinion of some metal analysts, the price of copper reflects how the economy is going better than any other commodity. (This might be disputed by a Quaker Oats marketing expert, who says that sales of blueberry-muffin mix are the best guide to economic trends. In a moderately rising economy, people with marginal incomes buy less oatmeal and more blueberry-muffin mix. In a falling economy, they shift back to oatmeal.)

If the copper standard were put in place, obviously a lowering of the price of copper—through increased supply or government subsidy—would stimulate economic growth in those many and basic industries in which copper is used: housing, automobiles, and so on. A higher price for copper would dampen economic growth. Evidently the supply of copper is reasonably stable and widespread enough not to be subject to significant political manipulation.

Copper-standard advocates have solid historical, and even religious, backing. The copper standard was first established, according to one biblical expert I know, by King Solomon. According to my expert, Solomon took gold out of circulation, decked the walls of the temple with some of it (a better use than storing it in Fort Knox), surrounded himself with a pride of fourteen golden lions, and put out copper coins. With the power of his currency, and some help through conniving with Hiram, king of Tyre, the economy of Israel flourished, as did the copper mines.

With this accumulating evidence that we may be moving toward a monetary system based on a single commodity, and that commodities other than gold or copper may be considered, and that the blueberry-muffin indicator may not be accepted, I think that we should look to some other commodity as the monetary base.

Two deserve attention. One is advocated by a nutritionist, agrarian, and supporter of the Henry George single tax. He proposes a protein-based monetary system, since, he points out, protein is the essential element of living cells. He would base the monetary system on a chicken-egg-protein base. Instead of fixing the price of eggs in dollars and cents, he would fix the value of the dollar in equivalent egg-protein units.

Another commodity that better meets the traditional standards for a good money base (and that is not easily subject to economic or political manipulation) is diamonds. No ordinary, natural diamonds, mind you, but Wellington diamonds, also called "Wellington fakes," which are manufactured and distributed by Madame Wellington and described not as "simulated" or "artificial" but as "counterfeit" diamonds.

The Wellington has these attributes:

- It has intrinsic value. If production and raw material costs are considered, a Wellington unit is more valuable, and of more stable value, than a natural diamond.
- The value of the Wellington can be maintained without the intervention of the international diamond cartel that now controls diamond prices.
- Like gold, the Wellington is not subject to destruction by moth or rust, and it is widely, if not quite universally, desired. The Wellington is meeting a rising demand, reflecting changing social and business mores. A Wellington sales report notes that the diamonds are bought principally by independent, self-employed, or professional women, and by men of some maturity, who either do not believe that diamonds and love are forever, or believe that if love is true, it can be sustained as well by a Wellington as by a natural diamond—if the setting is good.
- The Wellington passes the standard of "storing value." It has been demonstrated, especially during the recent period of inflation, that neither gold nor natural diamonds have been a reliable and stable investment. Not so the Wellington, which can be turned in by dissatisfied customers, who are guaranteed a natural diamond of the same size in exchange.

In sum, if our economic gurus are determined to adopt a monetary system based on a single commodity, they would do well to abandon their single-minded attention to gold and to consider any of several other commodities, not the least of which is Madame Wellington's diamonds.

WHAT DEBT?

(*Commonweal*, JANUARY 30, 1987)

The fears of federal deficits, of the imbalance of trade, of rising national debt seem to have gone the way of the herpes scare. They get some attention on television discussion programs but are no longer emphasized, and seldom mentioned, on the evening news.

Economists, generally, continue to express some concern over them, but with restraint—almost as though they were hedging their bets, or their professional reputations.

International businessmen, bankers, and other traditional defenders of the capitalistic system seem only slightly disturbed over conditions that used to keep them awake at night. Some even see virtue in current and prospective debts, deficits, and trade imbalances. The same is true of publications such as *The Wall Street Journal* and *Forbes* magazine.

President Ronald Reagan, who, in his first inaugural address spoke of how "for decades we have piled deficit upon deficit, mortgaging our future and our children's future for the temporary convenience of the present," seems less and less concerned about the national debt, or at least about the $900 billion increase that has occurred in the five years he has been in office.

One can fairly ask, "Why?" What are the reasons for these apparent changes of position and for the tolerance of conditions once held to be intolerable? There are obvious surface explanations. The president continues to be popular. Interest rates have gone down from the inordinately high level they reached in the Carter administration. The rate of inflation, which reached 13 percent a year in the last year of the Carter administration, is now about 4 percent a year (a rate once considered unbearable). Although the ship of state and of the economy may be losing way and settling slowly in the water, there is no water in the first-class cabins, and the deck is level.

There are deeper, more fundamental reasons for the acceptance, even the defense, of debt, deficits, and imbalances by bankers, businessmen, and their counselors and political representatives.

One major reason, as they see it, is that under pressure of budget deficits and mounting debt, liberals are in retreat and domestic programs are being cut back. Second, they see that capital (of the classical land-labor-capital trinity) is gaining in its advantages, both relative and absolute, over the other factors of production.

Those who control capital, and profit from that control, note a growing advantage over labor. Unemployment hovers at about 7 percent, a point at which labor analysts say management can effectively control wages and worker benefits.

The trend of wages in recent years has been downward. Average weekly wages of private, nonagricultural workers in the United States were $189 a week in 1977. Measured in 1977 dollars, the value of their weekly wages in 1985 was a little over $171, a decline of $17 dollars a week. Downward pressure on U.S. labor is further intensified by the importation of foreign labor, legal and illegal, and by bringing in (in the name of free trade) both raw materials and manufactured goods produced by low-wage workers in countries such as Taiwan, South Korea, China, and India. A recent news program showed steel workers in India, reported to be earning one dollar a day, producing manhole covers for Baltimore, Maryland, a city that does have a steel mill, or did have one. Goods are also coming in from countries such as West Germany and Japan, which have built-in indirect subsidies, in that their production costs do not include taxes of the magnitude of those paid by American workers and industry, much of it committed to the defense of those countries.

The pressure on American labor is further increased by competition from new equipment, plants, and automated machinery developed, built, and put in place with the aid of investment credits, tax-exempt industrial bonds, and other subsidies from federal, state, and local governments.

Capital also has an advantage, currently, over the second of the classical factors of production, namely, land and natural resources. Agricultural prices generally have been depressed. In the United States, farm prices, set against the prices of 1977 as an index base, are at an index number of seventy-nine. The prices of most industrial minerals—iron ore and copper, for example—are depressed, as are timber prices. Oil is now under severe downward pressure. Environmental protection is on hold.

More significant than these advantages are the integral advantages being given to capital and to the income on it, within the economic-political system itself.

Capital and income on capital have progressively achieved a preferred position in the United States, to the extent that capital income, at least for tax purposes, now has a status bordering on the sacred monies of the temple in ancient times. Capital is developing and propagating its own theological and philosophical support. Established religions are finding that they can accommodate capitalism to their theological and moral doctrines. Fundamentalist preachers are moved to take their religious-economic beliefs into politics. At least one conference on "Capitalism and the Constitution" has been scheduled. Many more are likely to follow during the observance of the 200th anniversary of the adoption of that document.

Now even the deficits and the national debt, it is seen, can be made to serve the interest of capital control and concentration. In fact, the transfer of more control over capital to those who now control it will be facilitated by the increase in the national debt. If, as is anticipated, the total national debt by 1995 will be close to $4 trillion, about three-fourths of which will be held by individuals of wealth (foreigners and Americans) and by financial institutions and other corporations, the annual cost of servicing that debt will approximate $400 billion. The federal government will then be, as it is now in lesser measure, the instrument through which taxes levied largely on earned income—that is, wages and salaries—will be collected, transferred, and transformed into capital, or into investment-producing capital gains and other tax-privileged forms of income. This all contributes to the continuing concentration of wealth, and power over wealth and wealth production—which may explain why the currently most popular investment in the United States, possibly in the world, is in future tax collections of the U.S. government.

NO SPREAD

FOR RED BREAD

(*New Republic*, AUGUST 22, 1981)

During the Vietnam War, spokesmen for the administration of President Lyndon Johnson reassured the nation periodically with the assertion that the strength of the U.S. economy was such that we could have both guns and butter. Evidently they meant these to be words of assurance that the war would require no serious sacrifice of "the good things" of life, and that consequently no one need be too concerned about the war itself. Robert McNamara went beyond the first level to say that we could have two wars like that in Vietnam and still have butter.

The guns-and-butter issue is back in the news, this time in more

involved context. It involves the USSR and includes not only butter but also bread, although butter is the critical component.

On June 9, the Reagan administration announced that it was lift-
ing the grain embargo imposed on the Russians by President Jimmy
Carter after the Afghanistan invasion, and that it would allow the
Soviet Union to buy up to 9 million tons of U.S. wheat and corn.
At about the same time, the administration announced that it in-
tended to sell surplus butter to foreign countries—evidently, in the
original proposal, including the USSR. Enter the secretary of state,
Alexander Haig, who has not been heard from much in recent weeks.
One White House source, unidentified in the press, said Haig was
"eloquent and convincing."

"No butter to the Russians" is the message; anything else would
be "sending the wrong message" to the Soviets, top advisors to the
president believe. The Russians can eat bread made from United
States wheat, spread with oleo made from United States corn, but
no butter made from United States cream. Evidently the use of
butter is the break point between a free society and a totalitarian
one, and Haig intends to hold the line—or, better, maintain the
spread.

This Haig policy runs contrary to the theories of some Sovietol-
ogists, who hold that the communist system can be broken down
more quickly and easily by exposing Soviet citizens to the good
things of Western civilization. Senator Robert Taft, the elder, was
one who held this point of view. Later advocates urged our government to encourage and help in establishing an automobile industry
and culture in the USSR, thereby getting the Russians hooked on
automobiles and, at the same time, because of the cost of maintaining that culture, significantly reducing the Soviet potential to
support a large military establishment.

Haig may know something about the power of butter as an instrument in high-level diplomacy. Evidently he thinks that butter,
in use in the Soviet Union, would strengthen the hold of the Communist party over the country, and possibly strengthen the belief
of the people in the system.

It may well be that the craving of the king in the nursery rhyme, who insisted that all he wanted was "a little bit of butter" for his bread is universal, marking the peoples of free, democratic, non-monarchical societies, as well as those of totalitarian communist societies.

The administration has taken note of some of the problems of controlling the ultimate disposition of butter once it enters the channels of international trade. There is a possibility that butter, like weapons, may be sold by the original purchaser. Poland is a country in point. In April 1981, the United States provided $73 million worth of dried milk and butter. Such butter, or more, sold under the new restricted policy of no-butter-to-the-Soviet-Union, might be shipped through.

The difficulties facing Haig and the State Department are not wholly new. In a somewhat different form and context, they had to be dealt with by the United States government in the early sixties after the United States had cut off sugar imports from Cuba and had to import sugar from other countries. The protectors of American security and integrity at that time insisted that no communist-produced sugar should be imported into the United States.

All seemed to be going well. The Cuban quota was filled by non-communist countries, including a few dictator-controlled ones. Included in the allocation was a small quota from Ireland—one boatload of 10,000 tons, as I recall. The reasons for this allocation were never clearly explained, but since the amount was so small, members of Congress let it pass, unchallenged, despite a few rumors that some of President John Kennedy's relatives in Ireland raised sugar beets. Then it was discovered that Ireland, while preparing to ship Irish sugar to the United States, was at the same time importing communist sugar from Poland. (At that time, Polish communism was less popular than it is today.)

The controversy was settled when the Irish promised that the sugar shipped to the United States would be pure Irish sugar, raised in the "Old Sod," processed and handled by noncommunist Irish, and therefore fit for American consumption. The Irish would themselves consume the communist sugar and take their chances on the consequences.

Quite possibly the State Department could demand similar commitments from any country to which we sell butter.

SPARE PARTS BECOME

AN INTERNATIONAL FORCE

(Culpeper News, JUNE 9, 1983)

A friend of mine recently bought a secondhand Mercedes-Benz. Having had, over a period of a month, my American-made and American-named car in various garages in an attempt to find out why, at about fifty miles an hour, a vibration of serious proportions developed somewhere in the car and was transmitted to the steering wheel, causing it to shudder, I asked him what he did about repairs and spare parts. He said that he might have some trouble finding a good repairman, but that a supply of spare parts was included in the original sales contract on the Mercedes, and that guarantee was transferred to him with his ownership, even second-hand.

In the course of a week's reading, after my conversation, I noted two references to the importance of spare parts—not in international trade, particularly, but in foreign policy. The first—a report out of India—charged that the government of the United States has been holding up the supply of spare parts for India's American-built atomic power plant in order to force India to conform to U.S. desires on nuclear policy. This action, the Indian government says, violates a U.S. obligation to provide spare parts for the power plant.

A second report, on the state of the economy in Cuba, contains the information that whereas Cuba now conducts most of its trade with socialist countries, it must do at least $100 million business with Western countries so as to get the spare parts necessary to maintain machinery previously purchased from those countries.

In the years since the end of World War II, as the United States has continued to be a major arms supplier to many countries of the world, the power of spare parts has not gone unnoted. Advocates of arms sales have been quick to point out the continuing, although limited, control over possible military actions by the purchasers. Evidently no Mercedes-Benz–type guarantee goes with military sales.

The power of spare parts has not, however, been fully exploited. If we had been alert to this power, it is possible that the building of a Ford plant in the USSR and also a Firestone tire plant—which were proposed and then turned down by the Eisenhower administration—might have been approved with the provision that spare parts and replacements had to be shipped from the United States, or manufactured with our approval, and that no improvements on the products could be made without American approval.

A Soviet Union hooked on the automobile culture, as we are, would be a Soviet Union with its military spending potential significantly reduced, and Russians driving Pintos of the original design and riding on unstable Firestone 500s might well have developed a serious sense of uncertainty, and possibly less militancy.

Nor has the potential of the spare part, as a means of limiting nuclear armaments, been fully exploited—although one or two of the more penetrating nuclear arms thinkers are coming closer to recognizing it.

One proposal, reportedly supported by Henry Kissinger, would attempt to break the deadlock on arms negotiation and reduction by first doing away with multiple-warhead missiles. The new rule would be one-bomb-per-missile. Since in most cases the missile launchers can be used more than once, the one-bomb-per-missile could be followed by a one-launcher-per-missile rule, with agreement that no launcher could be used more than once—as is the case with the oak barrels used for making bourbon in the United States. The barrels are resold and used for making Canadian whiskey.

Old launchers, possibly, could be sold to second-class countries, who might be allowed to have launchers and bombs, but no missiles. The USSR and the United States might further agree, as a means of limiting the destructiveness of nuclear war, to make no spare parts for their own launchers or missiles. The uncertainty over having working equipment might provide the essential deterrent to a nuclear war.

In any case, the importance of the spare part has been recognized by the Russian poet Andrei Voznesensky who, in a poem about queueing-up in Russia, wrote, "I am 47 for spare car parts (they signed me up at birth)/no. 1000 for a new car (signed up before birth)."

PROTECTIONISM
AND THE TRADE DEFICIT:
THE CONSUMPTION STANDARD
(1987)

Financial journals, commentators, the business sections of most major newspapers, for years now, have particularly emphasized the U.S. trade deficit, noting its threat to orderly trade among the more or less free-trade nations. On October 20, 1986, *The Wall Street Journal*, for example, saw the trade deficit as having displaced the global debt crisis as the "number-one" threat to the world economy. It saw protectionism in the United States on the horizon, especially advocated by presidential candidates and Congress.

Economists, too, express great concern. Alan Greenspan, in a recent statement, warned that West Germany, Japan, and the United

States will have to move quickly to narrow the trade gaps, or "the currency markets will do it for us." Evidently Greenspan and other establishment economists do not accept that in this case, market forces should be allowed to run freely. They are against "protectionism" but for "affirmative action" of a more general, financial nature.

The advocates of the simpler and more direct kind of protection argue that the old standards for determining what is fair and what is unfair in international trade are not being applied. The opponents of that kind of simple protectionism say that the old standards are no longer applicable.

If international trade is to be "fair," obviously there is a need to find other standards of judgment. Almost every day the press carries articles and editorials indicating what those standards should be. *The Wall Street Journal* also reported (December 17, 1986) that to the dismay of the United States (especially as it bears on the trade imbalance), Europeans (especially the West Germans) are resisting our urging that they spend more. The case of one German was given as an example of the resistance. When this German's Volkswagen Beetle failed to pass a federal automobile inspection, the owner said that he would not consider borrowing money to buy a car. "Better to walk than to borrow," he said. Washington, meanwhile, continues to urge West Germany and other European governments to give their citizens more pocket money through lower interest rates and tax cuts. They will then spend more on consumer goods, even to the point where they will go beyond buying nationally produced goods and begin to "buy American," as Bob Hope urges us to do. Germans, it seems, are not even "buying German." At the same time, Americans are being urged to "buy new cars," even to "buy German," and are in fact doing so—BMWs, Mercedeses, Audis, and to a lesser degree Volkswagens.

The Japanese, like the West Germans, are also uncooperative consumers. In their case, it is not so much automobiles as food. Jim Fallows, in a November 1986 article in *The Atlantic*, notes that most Japanese are thin. Fallows reports that the average American ingests 800 calories a day more than does the average Japanese—3,393 calories to 2,593. Allowing for some natural differences in size, this is still a significant difference and may explain why the average American is approximately twenty pounds overweight. Meanwhile, the Japanese market for American rice and soybeans is severely restricted.

Overeating, and being overweight, have been democratized in the case of the United States. We are the greatest popular overeaters and overconsumers in the history of the world, with possibly two exceptions: the Ik, an African mountain tribe whose members, by report, gorge themselves on a good day's kill without thought for other people, or for their own tomorrow; and the Romans, who overconsumed but did not put on weight by providing the vomitorium as an adjunct to the dining room. Sales of over-the-counter emetics are increasing in the United States.

Today, "We the People," as noted by Ronald Reagan in his State of the Union message, make up 5 percent of the world's population, yet we consume 25 percent of the world's production of fossil fuel. Overall annual consumption of material resources by the United States is more than twice that of Western Europe, four times that of Eastern Europe, and cannot even be compared realistically to consumption in other countries and areas of the world.

We have 5 percent of the world's population and we have 50 percent of its automobiles—one car for every 1.8 persons. Approximately 15 to 20 percent of our material production is used to pay for the construction and maintenance of these automobiles and 15 percent of the world's annual production of petroleum is used each year to fuel them. In an eight-hour day, the average American works approximately one and one-half hours to support his automobile. It has been suggested that any person who steals an automobile in the United States should be punished by having to support it.

Yet, the world evidently is not satisfied with our performance. We are being asked to consume more: Arab oil producers want us to use more oil in order to stabilize the Middle East. Japanese, Korean, and West German automobile producers urge more of their cars upon us, even using American parts as a sales aid. Argentines and Australians ask us to consume more beef and mutton. Brazilians and Colombians urge more coffee consumption on us; South American, Central American, Caribbean, and Pacific sugar producers would have us use more sugar; Asian, Middle Eastern, and South American producers of drugs continue to supply the American market.

Obviously, these and similar nations will just have to consume, or overconsume, their share of the world's production and throw away the excess. However, if they are unable to do so, their excess should be excluded from the U.S. market, especially if it involves grave threats to the personal health and safety of American citizens. For example, our duty on imports should reflect the differential between the percent of gross national product spent on defense by the United States and that spent by other countries or organizations, especially those that we are obligated by treaty and agreement to defend—notably, NATO, Japan, Taiwan, South Korea. If we are to be overdefended, so should they. They should bear their share of the overdefense.

If our highways are overcrowded and dangerous, theirs should be as crowded and dangerous; if there is insufficient space for highways, as in Japan, they should still be required to continue buying cars until their car-to-person ratio is comparable to ours. Falling short of that, they should pay a duty on any of their cars exported to the United States. They could produce a car that runs in place— since, by report, the Japanese run in place because there is too little room for jogging.

Similar standards should be applied in other areas. Citizens of countries exporting manufactured goods to the United States should be required to be overweight in roughly the same proportion as Americans, providing a market for American agricultural products. If not, they should pay a penalty for their own or their government's self-discipline.

Obviously, countries that export goods to the United States and still have the six-day work week (Japan and West Germany) should be penalized on two counts: (1) the excessive production of goods on the sixth day; (2) the underconsumption of goods because they have only one free day a week for leisure activities and leisure consumption.

We should force on the world the U.S. principles of production and consumption espoused by Henry Ford. He decided that workers should be paid enough (five dollars a day) so that they could buy what they were producing; that they should only work eight hours a day, so that they would have time to drive to work and therefore use cars; and that they needed a two-day weekend, so that they would be more strongly motivated to earn enough to buy a car that they could use for both days of leisure.

The U.S. tariff should exclude those goods that unfairly compete with the goods produced in the United States because of underconsumption and overproduction in the offending countries. If we are to become the supreme consumers for the world, then we should be paid by the rest of the free world for our consumption. This is the ultimate protectionism.

Part III

OF MEDIA, MESSAGES, AND
MISCELLANEOUS

IS AMERICA

THE WORLD'S COLONY?

(*Policy Review*, Summer 1981, edited 1988)

Albert Schweitzer said that if a civilization loses its ability to foresee and to forestall, it is headed for trouble. Is the United States
now losing its independence, its control over its own resources,
and even its military strength? Is it becoming, in effect, a colony
to the world?

In August 1980, a subcommittee of the House Committee on
Interstate and Foreign Commerce held hearings on direct foreign
investment in the United States. Direct investment is defined as
that which gives control over business or finance to the investors,
either through direct ownership or through control of stock hold-

ings. Direct investment in the United States, though not yet significant, had increased markedly, and tripled between 1970 and 1978. The ratio of foreign investment in the United States to U.S. investment abroad increased from 17 percent in 1970 to 29 percent in 1978. On a percentage basis, foreign direct investment in the United States increased by 99 percent between 1973 and 1978, compared with an increase of only 66 percent for U.S. investment abroad.

Since that time, the trend toward greater dependency on foreign investments has continued. Our trade deficits have continued, as have the deficits in the federal government, thus encouraging and attracting foreign investment in both private and government securities. In 1980 U.S. government debt to foreigners stood at about $121 billion, and annual interest payments to foreigners were $12 billion. By September of 1987 the debt had increased to $268 billion, an increase of more than 120 percent, and interest payments for 1987 on the debt approached $24 billion.

The growing dependence of the government of foreign borrowing was paralleled by developments in the private sector. In the third quarter of 1987, for the first time in more than fifty years, foreigners earned more on their U.S. investments than Americans earned on investments abroad—a shortfall of $267 million. In 1986 the Commerce Department reported that foreign-held assets in the United States exceeded American-held assets abroad by $263 billion.

According to the same report, in 1986 foreigners held more than $309 billion worth of corporate and other non-federal bonds in the United States, and U.S. banks reported liabilities of $449 billion, an increase of $94 billion over the previous year.

It is not only the amount of the investment that is important; so, too, is its concentration. Japanese investments accounted for the largest increase in direct investments: 166 percent between 1973 and 1978. Japan has become, by quantitative monetary measure, the leading economic imperialist in the world. By the end of 1986, Japan was a net creditor by $250 to $300 billion. Most of the Japanese holdings are in the United States, which has been able to run both its trade deficit and its federal government deficit because the Japanese have been prepared to pay the bill, in exchange for claims against the assets and profits of U.S. businesses and against future U.S. tax collections. There has also been a shift in the industrial composition of foreign direct investment in the U.S. Although manufacturing—principally oil and automobiles—maintains the lead, there has been a shift to trade, both wholesale and retail, with investment in such companies as Grand Union, Stouffer Corporation, and Beech-nut, dealing in products of everyday use. A growing trend can be seen toward investment in manufacturing industries in the Southeast. Nor is the initiative all on the part of investors. Communities and governments in the United States have been searching for foreign investments and offering favorable tax treatment, facilities financed through the issue of government tax-exempt bonds, and other enticements. One of the members of Congress indicted in the Abscam incident was tempted in part by the prospect of bringing foreign investments into his home state.

As noted in the 1980 congressional hearings, foreign investment has significance beyond questions of taxes, equity, and even economics. Foreign investment must be considered in the broader context of what, for want of another term, can best be called *neo-colonialism.* This form of colonialism is different in form and historical identification from the colonialism of the past, but it is substantially the same.

Like classical or traditional colonialism, neo-colonialism is marked by several salient features. The first is increased investment leading to control of the colonial economy from outside. In the case of the United States, control is exercised not by an imperial mother country, but increasingly by a number of foreign countries entering a relatively free investment field. All the same, with investment comes control.

For example, U.S. government efforts to prevent the export of U.S. technology, such as forbidding the sale of sophisticated computers to France (when France was suspected of intending to use the computers to help build a nuclear bomb), might well be undercut or circumvented if the technology could be exported under the protection or immunity of a multinational corporation with direct investments in U.S. companies. It should be noted that the U.S. does restrict direct foreign investments, to some extent, in minerals, communications, air transport, nuclear energy, and inland shipping activities, although foreigners are generally permitted to purchase noncontrolling interests in voting stock in companies operating in these restricted fields. During the 1950s and 1960s, the United States government did intervene in the USSR on the grounds that Soviet military potential might be advanced by such facilities.

The importance and dangers of foreign control over U.S. economic interests were made clear by the president of a major oil company during the oil embargo of 1973. He reported that his company had, in fact, allocated a larger share of the company's foreign oil production to the United States during the embargo than would have been warranted on the basis of each country's share of business before the embargo. Had he not been an American, or had his company not been controlled by Americans, it might have been much more difficult for him to have made the decision favoring the United States.

A second characteristic of neo-colonialism that is beginning to mark U.S. trade relationships is our growing role as a supplier of raw materials and as a purchaser of manufactured goods. The British established and maintained such a trading relationship during the U.S. colonial period, and it was one of the grievances that led to the American Revolution. Today, however, we ship timber to Japan and import fiberboard; we ship scrap metal to Japan and import automobiles; we ship coal to West Germany and import petrochemicals.

A third characteristic of the new colonial status is the absence of full control over the domestic monetary system. For a variety of reasons, the United States has lost full control over its money—witness inflation and a highly unfavorable balance of payments. Formal acknowledgment of this took place in the Nixon administration, when the dollar was devalued and allowed to float, subject to the pressures of the international money markets. Dollar instability might be even worse if other countries did not have large dollar holdings and therefore an economic interest in stability. But, as dollar holdings of OPEC countries continue to increase, so does the possibility of manipulation of the dollar—especially if the OPEC countries carry out their threat to base OPEC prices on a basket of currencies rather than exclusively on the dollar.

The neo-colonial status of the United States is also evident in noneconomic areas. For instance, U.S. military forces are now expected to defend other nations. In fact, in some cases the United States is under contract by treaty to defend other countries, notably West Germany and Japan. And, within the last three decades, without clear contract or treaty obligation, our military forces have defended the South Koreans and the South Vietnamese. Under the Eisenhower Doctrine, U.S. forces are committed to respond to requests from governments that believe themselves threatened by communist takeover. Is not the role of U.S. troops in these instances comparable to that of colonial mercenaries, although in this instance the countries calling on the colonial troops do not even pay the costs—except marginally in the cases of West Germany and Japan?

Under these conditions, our foreign military policies can be imposed from the outside. This is a clear historical example of what Charles de Gaulle defined as a state of dependency or colonialism. De Gaulle's point was that a first-class nation should never allow a foreign policy or military policy to be imposed upon it, and that when foreign policy or foreign commitment (in de Gaulle's case, it was French involvement in Algeria) begins to weaken a nation, either physically or morally, then that foreign policy has to be rejected.

A second sign of noneconomic neo-colonialism is our growing loss of control over our own borders and over immigration. The great influx of people from Puerto Rico in the 1950s was wholly within the terms of treaty agreements. Nevertheless, that influx was disorderly and disruptive and accompanied by many social problems, especially in New York. The more recent and continuing serious problem involves illegal immigration from South and Central American countries, especially from Mexico. This immigration does not have the legal support of treaty agreement. Estimates as to the number of illegal immigrants from these countries and areas reach as high as one million persons a year. The failure to control illegal immigration from Mexico is defended by some on the grounds that strict enforcement of immigration laws, more vigorous and thorough patrol of the border, harsher penalties, and quick deportation would "provoke" Mexico and lead to unrest among Mexican-Americans already in the United States. Possibly such actions would be provocative, but such a possibility does not eliminate the reality of the movement of persons into the United States, without legal right by statute or treaty.

More recently there has been an influx of refugees and expellees from Cuba, along with an increase in the number of illegal immigrants from other Caribbean and South American countries. The shipping of criminals and other undesirable persons to colonies, such as those whom Castro has been accused of sending to the United States, has a strong precedent in the British colonial practice of sending criminals to Georgia and later to Australia.

A more subtle manifestation of neo-colonialism is the challenge to the status of the English language in the United States. There has been both a practical and a legal accession to demands that at least some parts of the country should become bilingual or multilingual.

Imperial nations traditionally impose—or try to impose—their languages on subject or colonial peoples, as did the Portuguese in Brazil, the Spanish in South America, the British and the French in their African possessions, and, in less successful efforts, the British among the Boers in South Africa.

The process is more subtle in the United States. It is being done in the name of civil rights, of good citizenship, and of economic and cultural equality. Yet it runs contrary to historical evidence of

methods. Seldom did he make the case for either policy or program on an ideological basis, although he was not indifferent to ethical and moral considerations. He was, with presidential concurrence, a great treaty-maker, but his treaty proposals were based primarily on historical conditions, rather than on ideological assessments and projections. The NATO commitment, the Marshall Plan, the Truman Doctrine, the aid programs to Greece and Turkey, were not against Communists in the abstract, but against historically identified Communists. Nor was the Korean War defended as an involvement based upon a general policy of the containment of communism, but as an action directed toward carrying out World War II in the Asian theatre. The Acheson-Truman conception of national defense was one of a defined perimeter, described simply by President Truman when he said that any time a pig stuck its snout under your tent, the thing to do was to hit it on the snout. This foreign policy was classical, therefore restrained and limited.

Following the Truman administration, and the departure of Acheson, foreign policy came to be dominated by the ideas and historical philosophy of John Foster Dulles, secretary of state under President Dwight Eisenhower. Dulles had committed himself to foreign service early in his life and seemed to look upon that service almost as though it were a religious vocation. His approach to foreign policy was essentially moralistic and ideological. Communists were not to be treated primarily as nationalists, but part of monolithic world communism. In contrast with the limited and defined objectives of Truman and Acheson, Dulles's objectives were open-ended and global. Even "neutralism" was, in his view, "immoral." The line between non-Communists of all kinds and Communists of all kinds was clear to Dulles.

Dulles, like Acheson, was a treaty-maker. His treaties, for the most part, in contrast with those engineered by Acheson, were not limited to defined historical situations and geographical areas, but encompassed things that had not yet occurred, and might never occur. They transcended territorial limitations, reaching out for ideological conflicts that might arise in the future. In this spirit, and in anticipation of trouble, he supported the Southeast Asia Treaty. He advocated adherence to the proposals of the Military Committee of the Baghdad Pact, designed to put together an anti-Communist bloc in the Middle East, and was reported to have sought a combination of African nations to contain Egypt and Gamal Abdel Nasser. He supported passage of mutual, anti-Communist defense treaties between the United States and South Korea, the United States and Nationalist China, and one with Japan. Dulles was the great covenantor of modern times, combining in documentary forms both legal and moral obligations.

In addition to his bent for entering into treaties, Dulles was a great proponent of congressional resolutions—some to sustain current policies and governmental actions, others in anticipation. Whereas Truman went into Korea without special congressional support, Dulles, acting for President Eisenhower, was quick to come to the Congress for endorsements of administration commitments. Thus, he presented and secured the passage of the Far East (Formosa) Resolution in 1955, which he said put the Peiping government on notice that if it attacked Formosa, the United States would instantly be in the war.

Again in 1957, following the Suez Canal crisis, Dulles came to Congress asking for a joint resolution on the Middle East that would state the determination of the United States to assist any country in the Middle East that asked for help from threatened Communist-inspired aggression. (President Lyndon Johnson, following this precedent, sought and obtained the Tonkin Gulf Resolution in 1964.)

During the Eisenhower administration, the United States continued its policy of indirect intervention through supporting the French in Southeast Asia and by sending military advisors there. It also came to the defense of Quemoy and landed troops in Lebanon. Eisenhower's administration threatened retaliatory action against the British, the French, and the Israelis at the time of the Suez conflict, and planned the invasion of Cuba.

Meanwhile, secret, interventionist foreign policy was being carried on by the Central Intelligence Agency, directed by John Foster

Dulles's brother, Allen. Independent of Congress, not limited by treaty obligations or accepted standards for judging the methods by which international affairs might be conducted, the CIA enmeshed itself in foreign policy. It took credit for the overthrow of Jacobo Arbenz Guzman in Guatemala and of Mohammed Mossadegh in Iran, and acknowledged its involvement in anti-Communist activities in Laos, Vietnam, and other parts of the world.

Interventionism in the Kennedy and Johnson administrations was conducted under the guidance and inspiration of the secretary of state, Dean Rusk, a kind of Cromwell to Dulles's Calvin. Under Kennedy, the invasion of Cuba was attempted and some 17,000 special forces were sent into Vietnam. The CIA continued to be active in Southeast Asia and in Cuba.

President Johnson escalated the war in Vietnam into a major military engagement and sent troops into the Dominican Republic to "stabilize" the government. The doctrinal justification was based on a kind of amalgamation of the Monroe Doctrine and the Eisenhower Middle East Doctrine transferred to the West.

President Richard Nixon carried the Vietnam War several stages beyond the level that it had reached under President Johnson. New tactical and strategic measures were introduced, including what was called an "incursion" into Cambodia—the first incursion in our history, or certainly the first use of that word to describe a United States military action. It was an interesting choice of a word, since there is no verb form for incursion (as the verb *invade* goes with the noun *invasion*). One cannot incurse. An incursion is therefore existential, a kind of happening.

The Carter administration demonstrated its anti-Communist zeal and willingness to intervene by embargoing grain sales to the Soviet Union and by keeping United States athletes out of the 1980 Olympic Games because of Russian intervention in Afghanistan.

Although the Reagan administration has proceeded with a massive military buildup, and uses the violent language of cold war, its actual military interventions have been modest, although numerous. Libya was bombed. A few shells were fired into Lebanon by U.S. warships. Marines were sent into Lebanon, with no very clear mission, and subsequently withdrawn. Navy vessels, one of them the frigate *Stark*, were assigned to protect oil shipments in the Persian Gulf. Grenada was successfully invaded. Currently the United States government, or part of it, is supporting the Contra troops in Nicaragua, the Iranians, and possibly also Iraq in the Iran-Iraq War.

In *Democracy in America*, Alexis de Tocqueville observed that democracies find it very difficult to start a war and also very difficult to end one. His observations may be right about major wars such as World War I and World War II, or close to right, but they are not sustained by the U.S. history of military involvement since the end of World War II. In this period our military engagements have been marked generally by quick entrance and quick withdrawal, followed by prolonged diplomatic and economic conflict. These differences from de Tocqueville's theory are explainable.

The United States gets into war or military conflict more quickly than might be expected of a democracy because the preconditions for involvement are in place, ready and waiting for conflict. First, the ideologically defined basis, essentially anti-communism, elicits a response comparable to those political-religious conflicts of the past—between Muslims and Jews, Christians and infidels, Catholics and Huguenots, Puritans and Cavaliers.

Second, ideologically differing positions are sustained by treaties and agreements. Thus, President Johnson held that the Vietnam War, and our participation in it, was based on our obligations under the Southeast Asia Treaty Organization (SEATO). Doctrines and resolutions already in place further limit the need for presidents in office to make hard historical judgments before committing the United States to military action. In the Eisenhower intervention in the Middle East and in the Johnson escalation of the war in Vietnam, legality and obligation, it was argued, were based on historical decrees. The first case was supported by the Eisenhower Resolution on the Middle East; the other, by the Tonkin Gulf Resolution passed in 1964, long before the escalation, and also before the 1964 campaign in which candidate Johnson declared that he would not send American boys into Asia to do what Asian boys should do for themselves.

Third, presidential decisions may be further justified, and also insulated from historical reality and from congressional review, by the intrusion of presidential "doctrines," some sustained by congressional approval, others only by tradition or by the popularity or power of an incumbent president.

The two presidential doctrines that have had the clearest bearing on foreign and military policy are the Monroe Doctrine and the Eisenhower Doctrine, operating separately or in variable combinations.

The doctrinal approach to foreign policy began with President Monroe's statement of December 1823, when he declared that the American continents were not to be considered subjects for future colonization by any European powers, that the political system of the European allied powers was essentially different from that of America, and that any attempt on their part to extend their system to any portion of this hemisphere would be considered dangerous to "our peace and safety." The statement also promised that existing colonies or dependencies of any European power would not be interfered with and that in matters relating to European wars and other matters involving the European powers, "we have never taken any part, nor does it comport with our policy so to do."

Commentators and critics point out that the Monroe Doctrine was a mere declaration of presidential position, which in itself could not prevent intervention or commit the country to war without congressional declaration and support. Although the critics were undoubtedly technically and constitutionally right, the declaration subsequently took on doctrinal force, encouraging any number of succeeding presidents to interfere or threaten to interfere in South and Central American affairs. They did not seek congressional support, and they carried out their interventions with little fear of criticism or effective opposition.

The "doctrine" has been modified and has taken on new and

more comprehensive meanings with the passage of time. President
Eisenhower, with the passage of the Middle East Resolution in 1956,
was credited with having established a doctrine that stated that the
United States could intervene militarily in the Middle East if it
was asked to do so by a government threatened by Communist
takeover. The doctrine was not long confined to application in the
Middle East. It was combined with the Monroe Doctrine as a preliminary justification for the planning of the Cuban invasion and
for the Bay of Pigs venture. The basic political plan was that once
a beachhead had been established in a country, that government
would invite the United States to come to its aid because it was
being threatened by a Communist or Communist-inspired movement—in this case, the Castro government. An extension of the
Monroe Doctrine accepted that a foreign *ideology* could be treated
as an actionable threat, whereas a century or more earlier, the threat
had to be a foreign *government*. This defense was used to explain
and justify the intervention in the Dominican Republic by the
Johnson administration. Thomas Mann, the chief administration
spokesman for Latin American policy at the time, said that the
landing of U.S. troops in the Dominican Republic was not intervention but a "response" to the "intervention" of Communist sub-
versives. The Russians announced their version of the Eisenhower
Doctrine in the Brezhnev Doctrine, which justified their invasion
of Afghanistan because, by report, they were invited in to prevent
the takeover of a Communist-controlled government.

The Reagan administration's action in Grenada carried the combined Monroe-Eisenhower Doctrine a step further. There was no
invasion by a foreign country and there was no request by a non-
Communist government in power for help against Communists or
communism. The action seemed to be based on the proposition
that there should have been a request from a non-Communist faction and that there might have been one if such a faction had existed in Grenada, but since there was no such faction to make the
request, the Reagan administration could take the initiative. And
it did.

A fourth proposition that gives support to continuing intervention (once it has been initiated) attempts to justify (and insulate
from challenge) presidential or governmental military actions on
the grounds that the president in office is continuing policies and
programs initiated or carried on by a previous president or presidents. Although President Kennedy never offered continuity as an
official or personal defense for the Bay of Pigs operation, some of
his supporters occasionally pointed out that the plans for the invasion had been prepared by and for the Eisenhower administration. President Johnson used continuity as a defense of his escalation
of the war in Vietnam. He was, he said, only supporting and ad-
vancing a policy that had been supported by three presidents who
preceded him: President Truman, who had helped the French indirectly by giving them aid under the NATO program and the Marshall Plan while the French Indochina war was in progress; President
Eisenhower, who had sent in advisors; and President Kennedy, who
had sent in special forces and had given other help to the South
Vietnamese. President Nixon endorsed the concept of continuity,
saying that he was pursuing a policy that had been supported by
four previous presidents.

Intervention is also continued in a fifth way, during postwar periods, in countries where wars or military involvements have not
ended wholly to our satisfaction. Thus, in the defeat of Chiang K'ai-
shek by the Chinese Communists, although we were only indirectly and moderately involved on the losing side, we avoided
acknowledging failure by setting up and supporting a government
in exile on Taiwan for twenty years and refusing to recognize the
government of mainland China for nearly thirty years. In much the
same way, after the failure of the Bay of Pigs invasion, the United
States has refused to acknowledge diplomatically the existence of
Cuba, and for nearly twenty-five years has maintained an embargo
of Cuba's goods, thereby leaving that country's economy largely
dependent on Russian support. In the case of Vietnam, since the
ending of hostilities nearly fifteen years ago, we have followed a
policy of nonrecognition and of economic sanctions. If the China

quarantine of thirty years is accepted as the standard, openings to Cuba may be expected in about five years and to Vietnam in fifteen. If things do not turn out as we would like in Nicaragua, that country may expect to be under ban for thirty years, the subject of continuing harassment and direct or indirect interventionism. That could change if we begin to make both military and other foreign policy decisions with more relevance to historical realities, rather than to ideological distinctions and inherited doctrines, resolutions, and vague treaties.

LOOK! NO ALLIES

(*Foreign Policy*, Spring 1978)

American government officials, from presidents on down—as well as editors, political columnists, commentators, essayists, and historians—commonly assume that the allies of the United States include most members of NATO, Israel, Japan, Australia, New Zealand, and South Korea, plus some smaller countries scattered about the globe. But the fact is that the United States has few, if any, true allies. What it has instead is a number of nations that it maintains in a dependency relationship. This is a relationship that Washington has approved and cultivated—a relationship, in fact, that it insists upon whenever any of these dependents shows any sign of independence. Some of these nations truly were American allies in World War II. Others, such as Japan and West Germany, were added to the list later because they were no longer enemies, they needed the United States, and they were willing to accept the dependency relationship.

The German and Japanese surrenders after World War II were essentially unconditional surrenders, leaving those two countries militarily and (especially Japan) economically dependent on the United States. In reality, though, it was not only its enemies who surrendered to the United States after the war, but also its former allies in Western Europe. The North Atlantic Treaty was for them not so much an agreement among allies and sovereign nations as it was an acknowledgment of the economic and military realities of postwar Europe, a treaty of dependence—almost an unconditional surrender of a different sort to the United States. That is also what was required of other nations later added to the list of dependents, including South Korea, Iran, and, in a somewhat different context, Israel.

The vestiges of sovereignty and national self-respect that survived the formal NATO agreements were largely wiped out by Secretary of State John Foster Dulles's arrogant, moralistic domination of American relations with Europe as well as with non-European friends such as India and Egypt. Dulles generally proceeded without consulting, or even caring about, the opinions of other nations. He insisted that they (especially members of NATO) accept and support American policy.

He attempted to force the European nations into what he called a "European defense community," the effect of which would have been to require them to give up their last, limited claims to military independence. To push his plan, Dulles threatened an "agonizing reappraisal" of the American role in Europe unless his plan was adopted. He denounced Indian neutrality as "immoral." He forced the British, the French, and the Israelis to withdraw from Egypt at the time of the 1956 Suez War. Subsequently, unhappy with the Egyptians because they were not antagonistic enough toward the

Soviet Union, Dulles unilaterally decided—without consulting the European countries or the United States Senate, possibly without even consulting President Eisenhower—to pull out of the Aswan Dam project, thus leaving Egypt to the Soviets.

Although subsequent secretaries of state may not have acted as independently as Dulles, the presidents who followed Eisenhower showed great insensitivity to the dignity of allies. John F. Kennedy displayed indifference toward the British, especially Prime Minister Harold Macmillan, on the matter of missile deployment. Lyndon B. Johnson forced the Australians and South Koreans to send token forces to Vietnam. Richard M. Nixon ignored everyone, including the U.S. Senate, with his "incursion" into Cambodia; he and his agent, Henry Kissinger, negotiated a new relationship with China without even the slightest nod toward the obvious interests of Australia and Japan.

In 1964 Ronald Steel published a book entitled *The End of Alliance*. The book correctly perceived the changed realities in Western Europe: the altered relationships of Western European nations to each other, to the United States, and to other nations in the world. The one major defect was the book's title. What Steel had observed was not the end of an alliance at all, but the end of a dependency relationship. He noted the appearance of conditions and realities that required a reordering of relationships in NATO to reflect the growing independence, the self-sufficiency, and the desire for sovereignty among member nations. Those forces created pressures and demands that the NATO concept and form could not accommodate.

The first serious and open challenge to the old NATO concept— and the assertion, in fact, of a relationship much more like that of genuine allies—was made by Charles de Gaulle. When de Gaulle reemerged on the European scene in 1958, the way was open for the liquidation of France's Algerian commitment, for its escape from dependence on American aid to fight its foreign wars, and for the restoration of France in the military and economic complex of Europe. De Gaulle's return, and the recognition of the reality of France as a force in Europe—an independent force—caused concern in Washington. De Gaulle's conception of a united Europe, stretching from the Atlantic to the Urals—united not under a supranational political authority, but by free-choice arrangements among sovereign governments—challenged the prevailing U.S. idea of European unity. What Washington had in mind was political, economic, and military unity—a dependence on the United States and an alliance against the Soviet Union.

Fearful that the West Germans would move to support the French position, the United States tried to force them to make a choice between Paris and Washington. Various devices for sharing power were suggested in order to influence the West Germans to select Washington's policy. The most noteworthy was a proposal that would have at least made it appear as though there were a shared responsibility for nuclear defense in Europe and a European finger on the nuclear trigger. How the finger was to be selected was never made clear.

Europe rejected the idea of a multilateral or multinational nuclear force. The British and French particularly opposed it. Verging on the ridiculous was the American proposal for multinational forces and the mixed manning of vessels, ideas urged especially by Secretary of State Dean Rusk. One ship was sent out on a highly publicized voyage to demonstrate the feasibility of the concept. But this was undertaken even before there had been an agreement on whether the cuisine and the chef should be French, German, British, or American, or on who would select the evening movies, let alone on more weighty matters.

De Gaulle's announcement of his intention to withdraw the French forces from NATO's integrated military command was not an announcement that he was leaving an alliance, but rather a repudiation of dependency. As André Fontaine wrote at the time of de Gaulle's action:

> The arrogance of the president of the republic is disagreeable and
> even incomprehensible to his allies, but it is not the arrogance of an

isolated man, otherwise it would be only ridiculous. It is the arrogance of a man who is not resigned to anything which writes *finis* to
a nation about which history has spoken without a break for a thousand years.[1]

Four years earlier, in 1962, Raymond Aron, if anything an anti-
Gaullist, had explained:

It is an illusion to believe that the problems raised by General de
Gaulle will disappear when he no longer "graces the scene." The
privileged position of Great Britain in the atomic field is something
which will never be accepted in Paris, no matter who may be in
power. . . .[2]

The immediate American response was to try to isolate France from
the rest of Western Europe. With difficulty, the United States obtained agreement from the thirteen other NATO participants on a
common response to France. Yet the language of that response
showed not only the caution and reluctance of the Europeans about
agreeing to the American proposals for isolating France, but also
how much the United States was relying on concepts that had become irrelevant during the preceding fifteen years.

In effect, the United States took the position that its policy toward
Europe could be continued without France. The threat was that
Washington might actually abandon its efforts for a united Europe,
rather than accept any change in the elaborate structure of "military integration." Or NATO would simply pack up and move to
Belgium. Plans would be made around France. Undersecretary of
State George Ball, a leader of the move to isolate de Gaulle's France
or to force him to keep France within the NATO military structure, announced to the Senate Foreign Relations Committee at the
time that, "the NATO crisis is over. . . ." The other countries of
NATO, he said, were determined to press forward vigorously to

---

[1] André Fontaine, "What is French Policy?" in *Foreign Affairs*, October 1966.
[2] Raymond Aron, "De Gaulle and Kennedy: The Nuclear Debate" in *The Atlantic*, August 1962.

maintain the integrated military structure without France. In fact, it was much better from a military point of view to have French military power back on the continent of Europe, even though formally outside the NATO command and yet physically in Vietnam and Algeria. But not so for secular and theological legalists like Ball and Rusk.

Despite the early warning and other historical changes, the United States has persisted in honoring and adhering to the NATO concept. Washington has presumed its dominance—despite the French and British development of nuclear weapons; the French, British, West German, and Italian mastery of nuclear technology; the Greek declaration of some measure of independence from the United States by terminating homeport facilities for the U.S. Sixth Fleet; the restoration of democracy by the Portuguese without American help; and the new influence of Spain.

The United States remained generally indifferent to the opinions of so-called allies about events in other parts of the world. Most Western European nationals had grave doubts about the wisdom of American involvement in Vietnam. Some openly criticized it. But Washington paid little attention to their point of view, in much the same way that it ignored Japan's attitude and its interests in that war. Similarly, the United States now appeared to be indifferent toward Japanese opinions and concerns over the announced intention to withdraw American troops from South Korea in 1978. Presidential candidates regularly reflect this arrogance of indifference. "If elected, I will reduce troops in Western Europe," one will say. "If elected, I will withdraw troops from South Korea," another will declare.

Australia is another example of a nation that is called an ally but is treated as a dependent. For almost two decades following World War II, Australian foreign policy was symbolized by Sir Robert Menzies. He accepted the cold war as central to policy, and he gradually shifted Australian association and dependence from Great Britain to the United States, as British power waned and as Washington began to emphasize the threat posed by Asian communism to American interests—and also, therefore, to Australian interests. Australia was also somewhat fearful of the instability of the former colonial lands of the South Pacific that were becoming independent. The supposed alliance with the United States was formalized in the ANZUS Pact (Australia, New Zealand, United States) and on a more comprehensive scale by Australia's joining the Southeast Asia Treaty Organization (SEATO). Australia followed American policy direction almost to the letter. Australian troops fought in South Korea and Vietnam. Australia allowed the United States to establish bases and tracking stations on its soil. And Australia declined to recognize China.

Following Menzies's retirement in 1966, and in view of the growing disenchantment with the Vietnam War, Australia also began to develop a spirit of independence and to demonstrate that a new relationship existed. Prime Minister Gough Whitlam's Labor government, elected in 1972 after twenty-three years of Liberal party rule, withdrew Australian troops from Vietnam, protested the American bombing of Hanoi and Haiphong, and undertook to establish a changed relationship with China, quite independent of what the United States was doing or wanted done. Yet Washington proceeded as if the old relationship of dependency still existed. It continued to send ambassadors who reflected the attitude that Australia was a kind of semi-independent Texas populated by cattlemen, sheep farmers, cane-cutters, and beer drinkers who would be ready when called upon to serve American interests.

During the forty years since the state of Israel was established— with the support of the United Nations and of the major nations of the world, including the Soviet Union—the United States has gradually moved to make Israel almost wholly dependent on the American government. French and English interests were repudiated at the time of the Suez War, and the United Nations was allowed to shed its responsibilities almost without protest when it withdrew in the face of Egyptian threats before the 1967 war. The Soviets, too, had more or less removed themselves, leaving the United States as the chief supporter of Israel.

Progressively, the United States began to look upon Israel as a dependent and to treat it as such. Israeli ambassadors to Washington came to be selected on the basis of their good connections in the United States. Candidates for leadership in Israel had generally argued that they should be elected because of their support in the United States—until Menachem Begin suddenly took the position that Israel was a sovereign nation, an ally of the United States rather than a dependency. Distinct from his predecessors, Begin was not elected on the basis of widespread recognition or support among Americans. Rather, he believed that the United States has a political, moral, and even military interest in the independent existence of Israel. The establishment of the state of Israel was more than a humanitarian act. It was a political act, establishing a sovereign state of special character and purpose.

Begin, not unlike de Gaulle, declared that he would take the initiative in foreign policy, that he would seek to have not defensible boundaries but a defensible country, that he would not wait for a UN initiative relative to the problems of his country, or indeed wait for American initiatives or directions.

In contrast to its attitude toward allies, the United States has treated its enemies of the postwar years—principally the Soviets and the Chinese—with respect and deference. It confers with them. It keeps them informed on matters of critical common interest and warns them about things that might be controversial.

Washington accepts the fact that both these nations have nuclear bombs, and that Soviet nuclear armaments have been designed and justified for the exclusive purpose of countering or overcoming American military power. Yet Americans protest vigorously when nations that are defined as allies build bombs or test them, or when they build nuclear reactors for themselves or other nations for nonmilitary purposes. The protests are especially strong against developments that are thought to make proliferation of nuclear weapons easier, if not more likely.

Proliferation, as now defined, means the possession of nuclear weapons by more nations than now have them. This definition, of course, excludes the increase in number, quality, and kind of nuclear weapons by the two most active proliferators, the United States and the Soviet Union, both of whom now have more than enough nuclear power to destroy each other. A nation that is asked not to develop its own nuclear weapons might well inquire as to what the Americans and the Soviets intend to do with the bombs they do not need for deterrence or retaliation. If the Soviet Union and the United States had only enough nuclear weaponpower to offset each other, the argument for nonproliferation would have far more strength among other nations.

If one sets aside the substantive, historical, and ideological differences between the Soviet Union and the United States and looks only at American methods and procedures for dealing with them, one could fairly conclude that the American government tends to treat its enemies as if they were allies. Meanwhile, American allies are treated as if they were enemies—or, at best, as highly unreliable allies to be consulted as little as possible and expected to accept U.S. policies and support U.S. programs.

Obviously, the United States must adopt a new attitude toward, and develop new working relationships with, at least five countries—Australia, West Germany, Japan, Iran, and Israel.

The lopsided American relationship with Japan should be modified to give Japan fuller responsibility, and even more military autonomy. Japan is no military threat to the United States, or China, or any other country. Japanese military problems are largely defensive and possibly psychological. U.S. relations with Japan should not be based on pre-World War II conceptions or realities.

The same is true of West Germany—although, in the German case, the attitudes of other nations in Western and Central Europe, and of the Soviet Union, make any move toward giving West Germany military autonomy and significant strength more difficult to justify. American troops and American-controlled military power must remain the principal armed force in Western Europe. They function there as double hostages, to both the East and the West. The allied relationship with West Germany should take account of this reality and make room for greater German participation in policy decisions about the military forces in Europe, not to mention a greater West German contribution to their support. Indeed, perhaps the Soviets should also be asked to bear part of the cost of maintaining American forces in Europe.

Australia, too, deserves genuine allied status. It is one of the few countries in the world that has control of its own resources, both material and human. It is rich in critical raw materials and it is underpopulated. Like Japan and the United States, Australia is a country that can do more than deal with its own economic problems. It should be viewed as a potential contributor to and participant in policies and programs that bear upon political and economic conditions in the South Pacific, Southeast Asia, and China.

Australia's potential as an ally is probably limited. But it should be remembered that Australians fought valiantly in both world wars. More can be done to develop and integrate Australian naval and air power into whatever stable military structure is needed in the South Pacific. The country's real potential, however, is in its economic resources, and especially in its role in the orderly, constructive, and morally controlled use of its uranium resources.

Essential to any alliance is a shared purpose, perceived to promote the common good of members or participating nations—a common good that cannot be achieved as effectively by one nation acting alone or by two or three nations operating to the exclusion of others that have a vital interest in the goals of the combined effort. Nations participating in an allied effort need not have that perfect conformity of customs, habits, ideas, and manners suggested by Edmund Burke to be the real forces that hold nations together. But the greater this conformity, the greater the strength and durability of the alliance are likely to be. Movement toward such conformity among participants in an alliance is clearly desirable. Agreement on methods is also desirable, but even with differences and disagreements, alliances can and have worked. Certainly there were major differences, both as to strategy and as to tactics, among the allied commanders, including Dwight D. Eisenhower and Viscount Montgomery, in World War II—not to mention the major ideological differences between the United States and the Soviet Union. Yet the war was waged effectively, at least to the point of military victory.

Alliance allows for differences in function, and in physical, military, economic, and philosophical contributions. To be effective, alliance requires compromises and concessions, but only among nations whose sovereignty and integrity are clearly recognized. Without such recognition and respect, there can be no true alliance, only the appearance or the form.

Dependencies are dependencies, despite documentary declarations to the contrary. Allies are something else. There must be among them, with or without formal affirmation, a bond of intellectual and moral commitment. As Machiavelli admonished, the relationship of ally to ally is a better, more reliable, and more lasting one than that of patron to dependent or of conqueror to subject peoples. The United States needs allies, not dependencies.

IS IT A PARADOX?

OR JUST A DILEMMA

FUSING WITH A SYSTEMIC

CRISIS?

(*Washington Post*, OCTOBER 25, 1986)

Sunday, October 5, 1986, started off for me as a reasonably good day. The weather was fine. The front-page headlines and stories of the *Washington Post* were encouraging. The paper carried additional commentaries on the return of Nick Daniloff, the American journalist in Moscow who was arrested by the KGB. I was assured he was happy to be back in the United States and that he resented the Russians' having taken several days out of his life. (The only dissenting note I had heard on Daniloff's loss of time to the Russians was that of a television technician, who observed that his sympathy for Daniloff on this count was running out, since Daniloff had taken six days out of the technician's life.) The paper noted again that the tax bill was historic and monumental and that the forthcoming meeting of President Ronald Reagan and General Secretary Mikhail Gorbachev was cause for optimism. In the sports section, a Redskins victory over Dallas was predicted, and the right arm of Roger Clemens, the Boston Red Sox pitching ace, was reported to be well.

Then I turned to "Outlook" to be greeted by a headline declaring, "Reagan is Leaving an Ominous Legacy in Foreign Policy." Since Reagan will not leave the presidency for another two years, I was somewhat confused by the headline. Was he leaving the legacy before leaving the presidency? How does one leave a legacy before one has left?

Not sure what the headline meant, I went on to former national security advisor Zbigniew Brzezinski's text, to find that in his judgment, Reagan was "likely to bequeath to his successor an ominous global agenda." This ominous character is manifest in four areas of national security: the geostrategic, the regional, the economic, and the political. Evidently the "geostrategic" and the "regional" do not include economic and political concerns.

Having gotten by these depressing early observations, I found myself, as well as the country, as observed by Brzezinski, in additional difficulties. We are beset by paradoxes and dilemmas of various kinds—a startling paradox, a paradoxical presidential choice, sharper dilemmas, geostrategic dilemmas, and major regional dilemmas. Probably worst of all, said Brzezinski, is a current Central American dilemma, which is likely to fuse with a wider systemic crisis of Mexico. The image of a dilemma fusing with a systemic crisis is almost too much to bear.

Rereading the article searching for better understanding of the legacy being left, I became aware of the burden of the adjectives I was called upon to bear. "Assurances" were not just assurances, but "categorical"; a "likelihood" was not just that, but a "real likelihood." (Can there be an unreal likelihood, or a likely likelihood?) Partisan criticism was "carping." Standards were "conventional," as distinguished from, I assume, "unconventional standards," which probably cannot properly be called standards. "Concessions" must be "genuine," "reality" is "perplexing," "eagerness" is "excessive" (as it usually is, even without the adjective).

Presidential actions must not be merely "tangible"; they must be "more tangible" (than what? more tangible than "tangible"?). And so the adjectives run on, until they all but overwhelm the nouns to which they are attached, and remind one of the language of the fifties.

Amid all of these adjectives, things are happening, or about to happen. Regional conflicts are likely to "mushroom in intensity." I have never thought of a mushroom as intense and have difficulty imagining a conflict mushrooming in intensity. Along with the mushrooming is a "continuing and expanding intrusion of Congress into the tactics of foreign policy." Obviously, the author thinks that an expanding intrusion into tactics is dangerous.

Ironically or paradoxically or otherwise, many of our troubles, thinks Brzezinski, might have been prevented, or "mitigated," if "national security advisors had been elevated into the preponderant players exerting control from the White House." Underneath all the adjectives, then, this seems to be the key point: elevating a national security advisor into a "preponderant player."

THE FOUNDING OF
THE UNITED STATES

(Social Science Record, 1987)

The founding of the United States included three stages. The first was the Revolution, itself essentially a revolution against government with its purposes stated and justified in the Declaration of Independence. The Declaration was an expression of faith by the men who signed it. In 1922 Gilbert Chesterton declared, "America is the only nation in the world that is founded on a creed. That creed is set forth with dogmatic and even theological lucidity in the Declaration of Independence; perhaps the only piece of practical politics that is also great literature." The creed to which he referred was stated in these words of the Declaration:

that all men are created equal; that they are endowed by their creator
with certain unalienable rights; that among these are life, liberty,
and the pursuit of happiness. . . .

These words were not set down as part of a rhetorical exercise.
They were not used merely as a justification for a revolution, or as
an inspiration, but rather were intended to persist beyond revolution to become the foundation in belief upon which democratic
institutions of government were to be built. The men who wrote
and subscribed to the Declaration took what they had done very
seriously, for if the Revolution they proposed failed, they were in
danger of being shot or hanged. The Revolution "against government" succeeded; the language and thoughts of men such as Thomas
Jefferson, Patrick Henry, Thomas Paine, and other advocates of the
war were vindicated.

The next stage of the Revolution, following five years of confusion and instability under the Articles of Confederation, began with
the convening of the Constitutional Convention in 1787 and the
completion of the ratification process in the fall of 1788. This second stage has been called by Professor John Kaminsky of St. John's
University (Minnesota) "A Revolution in Favor of Government";
and such it was. The battle of rectification was fought between the
anti-Federalists, who clung to the precepts of nongovernment and
the antigovernment sentiments of the Revolution—men such as
Samuel Adams of Massachusetts and George Mason of Virginia—
and the Federalists, whose case was made primarily in the *Federalist Papers* by Alexander Hamilton, James Madison, and John Jay.

The men who participated in the drafting of the Constitution
were politicians. They acknowledged the reality of compromise and
anticipated that not everything they did would stand the test of
history. At the same time, they believed that the principles upon
which the new republic was to be founded were valid. They did
not look upon what they were undertaking as "The American Ex-
periment," as it is sometimes called, but rather as a test of reason
and as historical lessons being tested in a new context.

They did not consider that the intellectual and moral bases for their proposals came from especially gifted or chosen delegates in the convention, but rather that they were drawn from political history and philosophy. They were not "new" political thinkers, although most had some new ideas, but they were students of politics and of history. They brought to the drafting convention the wisdom and experience of ancient political thinkers as well as of those who, by their standards, were modern. Plato and Aristotle were at the convention, as were Montesquieu, Locke, Hobbes, Adam Smith, and Rousseau. Plutarch was there as a special resource both for history and for political theory, as were Thucydides and Tacitus. Contemporary, or nearly contemporary, historical sources also were used. Jay, for example, in the fifth essay of the *Federalist Papers*, quotes from a letter from Queen Anne of England to the Scottish Parliament in which she emphasized the union between England and Scotland as vital to peace. There are, in the Constitution, touches of Machiavelli, although he is not identified. And there is the continuing force of biblical thought.

The third stage of the founding process took but a short time but has had a long, continuing, and stabilizing effect on American life, politics, and government. In 1789, the first Congress, as had been promised by Federalists in their campaign for the ratification of the Constitution, proposed as amendments to the Constitution what has come to be known as the Bill of Rights. The congressional proposal was soon adopted by the states and has since been of utmost importance in preserving the personal liberties of the citizens of the United States, for whom it has been a kind of Magna Charta. Jefferson, a Federalist, might well have argued that the rights specified in the amendments were implicit in the revolutionary "inalienable rights." George Mason and Virginia were won over, and Jefferson summarized what had been accomplished in the third stage of the founding by observing that there had "been opposition enough to do good, and not enough to do harm."

WHO WON THE ELECTION?

(*December 1, 1982;* Edited March 1988)

Those who may try to determine the political significance of the 1988 election may be looking at an aspect, perhaps as I did in 1982, of secondary importance. The truly important struggle may be, as it was in 1982, among the three major television networks. The competition involved areas of measurable superiority or failure: (1) Nielsen ratings; (2) earliest predictions of the outcome of the election, either in individual contests or in overall gains and losses of the two parties; and (3) best scores of right over wrong predictions, with some adjustment and a greater margin of error allowed to networks making early mistakes than was allowed to those who persisted in error, or made late mistakes.

The Nielsen ratings were inconclusive, each network seeming to have attracted roughly the same number of viewers nationwide, with variations, possibly significant, among the major cities of the country. NBC won in New York, CBS won in Chicago, and ABC at least for a time was the leader in Los Angeles. This distribution seems to indicate a national pattern, moving westward. But that pattern, which might have been developed into a theory about election reports and the major networks, was broken by the fact that ABC won in Philadelphia and Detroit. There was no reported breakdown of network appeal, or distinctions among them, in the three north-south divisions of the country made by political analysts, namely, the Sunbelt, the Sleetbelt (this one not as clearly identified as the other two), and the Snowbelt.

Since the general indicators did not clearly distinguish successes or failures of the networks, they and some observers of television competition resorted to more qualitative, possibly more refined, standards for distinction. ABC claimed that it called the most gubernatorial and Senate races before its two rivals did. This is possible, but it leaves unanswered the question of how many wrong calls ABC made, and which calls ABC missed. One might say, if one knew the facts, what Mr. Dooley said to Hennessy, who was boasting over having foretold the Spanish-American War, "Y'er right, Hennes'y. Y've foretold ev'ry war in this half cen'ry, as well as many that've niver occurred."

NBC did not dispute the ABC tabulation of "first calls" but declared that once called by NBC, not one prediction had to be corrected. The big winner for NBC was its prediction of the victory of Governor James Thompson in Illinois. Evidently they took into account one fact of political reality, namely, that Richard Daley was no longer among the Democratic politicians in Illinois, and the late counts and lost-and-found ballot boxes of former days were not likely to figure in the equation. ABC and CBS may have been waiting for the Daley factor, which was supposed to reflect his belief that every citizen of Chicago, if not of Illinois, had a natural right to vote in at least twelve presidential elections and twenty-five gubernatorial elections in a lifetime—and that the number of votes remaining unused by any Democrat whose political life was prematurely shortened could be voted by the party.

CBS seemed to concentrate on the House of Representatives, dealing in large numbers and allowing itself a significant give-and-take for error, reducing its predicted number of Democratic gains from an early 34 ("give or take 9") to 31 ("give or take 7 or 8") to a 29 ("give or take 6") to a 1 A.M. 27 ("give or take 5"). All through the night, to its credit, CBS, speaking through Dan Rather or Bill Moyers, had warned the audience not to take the CBS predictions as final.

Each network seemed pleased with its heavy commentators. The ABC official said that David Brinkley was "extraordinarily connected with elections." The president of NBC News is reported to have beamed broadly at Tom Brokaw and Roger Mudd. And CBS either declared itself the psychological winner or was so declared. I do not know what the basis of that attribution or achievement was, unless it was the introduction and use of Texas images and metaphors (Rather, Moyers, and Bob Schieffer all being from Texas) in the commentary. Among the Rather contributions were such lines as: "He's gotta feel he's been rode hard and put away wet."

One race, he said, was "hatband tight," another "tight as a cinch strap," another "hot as a hickory fire," and one, slipping a little, "bonfire hot." Moyers was a little more general in metaphors, describing one contest as "a backyard hen fight," and another as having "as many threads as a Persian rug."

This was a heavy load of language to absorb in one election evening. The psychological consequences could be serious.

THE COMMUNICATOR
BECOMES THE OBFUSCATOR

(*Rappahannock News*, MARCH 5, 1987)

Public figures have been subjected by history, or by the press, to one-word or one-phrase characterizations. There was Pepin "the Short," then Charles "the Bald." Henry was "the Confessor," and Ivan "the Terrible." In naming current public figures, it may well be wise for the press to proceed carefully, to avoid and to reject any early or sweeping characterizations.

Candidate Walter Mondale, for example, was put in jeopardy of such characterization when his press secretary announced that Walter intended to "elucidate the American people," thus opening the way to his becoming known as "The Great Elucidator."

Lyndon Johnson, had he been careless, might have become known as "The Great Manipulator," Eisenhower as "The Great Procrastinator," Richard Nixon "The Great Dissimulator," and Jimmy Carter "The Great Vacillator."

Taking their inspiration from the historical label of Abraham Lincoln as "The Great Emancipator," the press, early in Ronald Reagan's first term as president, began calling him "The Great Communicator." What he was communicating was never made very clear either by the president or the press, but both seemed sure that he was communicating. The president seemed pleased with his title. Years ago, Marshall McLuhan, one of the first social philosophers to give serious thought to the impact of television on society, concluded that content in television communication was all but irrelevant, and that the Media was the Message. Ronald may well be the incarnation of the McLuhan observation; namely, the communicator who is the communication.

In anticipation of the president's 1987 State of the Union message, political experts, communications specialists, and commentators advised the public that the substance of the speech would not be important, but that they would respond to how the president looked and sounded. Graphics and sound would be of more significance than the ideas that might be included in the address.

The judgment of the experts after the speech—not quite a consensus but something like a general conclusion—was that the president looked good but had not sounded good; that the overall experience was somewhat like watching a television news program and listening to it, or trying to, when the picture was good but the sound was not.

In the president's case, whether he is better with a good picture and a bad sound or with a good sound and a less-than-good picture (if one can or must make the choice) has not yet been made the matter of thorough investigation.

The quality of television reception in Hawlin' Hollow, where my house is situated, is not predictably good, especially in the early evening, about the time the network news comes on.

When Walter Cronkite was the anchorman on CBS, I would as a rule watch him when the sound was bad and the picture good. Even without sound, Walter was acceptable. The soundness of my judgment was confirmed when I read that Walter was the most popular of the evening newscasters among the deaf. When the picture was bad but the sound good, I chose John Chancellor, when he was still the anchorman on NBC. When both the sound and the picture were bad, I went to ABC, as the news on that network was about as clear when sound and picture were confused as it was when both were clear. I have not worked out satisfactory rules for choosing among the current evening anchormen on the major networks.

As for the president, I think he is best when the picture is good and the sound good—like humming, good enough to be heard but not listened to. Because of the events affecting Iran and Nicaragua, and in a secondary way a number of other countries, many persons listened to the State of the Union message hoping for some explanation of what was going on. Listening to Reagan, however, can be distracting. One may be distracted trying to recall the source of his quotations: from former Democratic presidents? from old Gary Cooper movies? from the Constitution? from the Bible? If one studies the influence of speech writers, the distraction would be in trying to figure out what parts of the speech came from which speech writers, who, according to report, compete for presidential acceptance—or for the First Lady's acceptance.

Beyond the State of the Union message, whatever may be the cause, communications between the president and the country seem to be getting a little blurred. The president may need a new title before his term ends, possibly "The Great Obfuscator"—whether he obfuscates on purpose or simply because his public statements reflect the state of his administration. Possibly this all proves the truth of what has been said of the president (actually not said of him, but of someone else and applied to the president), namely, that "he imagines the past and remembers the future."

THE EX - KING IS TIRED,

LET HIM REST IN SILENCE

(*Washington Star*, MAY 19, 1977)

There has been, I think, excessive reaction among editors, commentators, columnists, and the media in general to the interviews of Richard Nixon.

In the first place, no one had to watch the programs or listen to them. The nation was not made into a captive audience, as it was for the Carter-Ford debates. All of the major broadcasting organizations carried the debates at the same time, leaving the nation no challenging alternative programs, such as "Charlie's Angels" or "The Six Million Dollar Man" or "Maude" to turn to.

For those who felt compelled to pay some attention to the Nixon interviews, there were at least three possible TV set adjustments that might have made things easier.

Those who don't like Nixon's looks, but were concerned about what he might say, could have blurred the picture and listened to the verbal exchange.

Those who are Nixon-watchers, but not listeners, could have turned down the sound and watched the face—in the manner of the poet Jay Meek, who has written of Nixon

> Gray jawed, barricaded in the White House
> The President has been watching television
> He has been watching himself too long
> His eyes click and roll like fruits
> In the windows of a gambling machine.

Those who, out of sense of duty or out of fear, thought that some "attention must be paid" could have blurred both the picture and the sound.

In the second place, there was nothing very surprising or newsworthy in the Nixon performance. He was acting in character. Discovering the real Nixon in the David Frost interviews is comparable to discovering the real Vietnam War, as the *New York Times* and *Washington Post* did, in *The Pentagon Papers*.

I think it unfair to charge, as some critics have, that Nixon gave the interviews because he was offered money. I believe that he would have done it without pay. He was not paid for his "Checkers" speech in 1952, or for the press conference after his defeat in the 1962 campaign for governor of California.

If Nixon had been Enoch Arden, after looking through the window and seeing the happiness of his former wife and children with her new husband, he would not have turned away and gone back to the sea forever. He would have tapped on the window until noticed. And he would have returned occasionally thereafter to tap on the window again and remind those in the house that he was outside, lonely, and suffering in the cold.

Our concern should not be with Nixon, but with the press and media response and with the need for institutionalizing procedures for dealing with presidents who resign, or are forced out of office, short of impeachment and conviction.

The writing press gave full cry and full coverage to the Nixon interviews, almost to the point of making it a case of "indecent overexposure." And the major papers, or "papers of record" as they call themselves, reprinted complete transcripts.

The networks were more restrained, but not out of some detached judgment as to the newsworthiness of the interviews. They were following the strange rules of television: withholding or restricting coverage of what is in essence a news event, if one of the other television networks or organizations has either paid for the news event or purchased the rights to cover it. Since Metromedia had bought the Nixon interview, the networks respected Metromedia's rights before, during, and after the act.

In much the same way, they respected ABC's purchased coverage of the Indianapolis 500 race. The other networks and media groups did not cover the race as a full news event until the postponed showing by ABC had taken place. There were hints on some of the news programs, mostly the local ones, that the race had been run, and that possibly someone had won. But there were no pictures. There was a hint or suspicion that the results would not be official until the race had been shown on ABC later in the evening.

One must wonder whether the networks that had not bought rights to televise a proposed invasion of Haiti some ten years ago would have respected the coverage rights secured in advance of the action itself by one network. One must wonder how they will cover the CBS-purchased interview of Nixon aide H. R. Haldeman—when and if that interview is held. While we wait, it is worthwhile to consider formalizing a procedure for dealing with presidents who resign from the presidency as Nixon did.

Sir James Frazer, the anthropologist, reported that as late as 1884, in one of Central Africa's Kingdoms, when the people had "conceived an opinion of the king's ill government, they sent a deputation to him with a present of parrot's eggs, as a mark of its authenticity, to represent to him that the burden of government must have so far fatigued him that they considered it full time for him to repose from his cares and indulge himself with a little sleep."

The king would then thank his subjects for their attention to his comfort, retire to his home as if to sleep, and there give instructions to his women to strangle him. This they immediately did, according to Frazer.

We need a modern, comparable, but civilized ritual—a proper notice to the president that the time has come for him to go; a modest and appreciative acceptance of the message by the president; a quiet departure, following his taking a vow of silence as to all political subjects; and a resolution on the part of the news media to respect his vow and to help him keep it.

TWENTY YEARS

ON THE RECORD

(Christian Science Monitor, MARCH 11, 1986)

On Monday, February 24, 1986 the twentieth anniversary of the Godfrey Sperling-*Christian Science Monitor* breakfast series was observed at a breakfast meeting at the Sheraton-Carlton Hotel in Washington. The attendance was good, as it should have been. The press was well represented, as was Congress. Officials ranging from Clark Clifford, who was a part of the Truman administration, to Caspar Weinberger, of the Reagan administration, were there. Tributes were well spoken, both to Godfrey and to the *Monitor.* Jokes, now a standard part of every Washington meeting, were told—some good, some bad.

The distinguishing characteristics of the Sperling breakfasts have been given too little notice. The first characteristic was that press attendance was limited to the writing press. The clutter and distraction of lights, cameras, and recorders were excluded. The guest was assured, therefore, that what he might say would get the attention of a listener and the further attention, unless the reporter trusted a long memory, of being recorded at least in written notes.

The second distinguishing characteristic was that the breakfast meetings were "on the record." This distinction is especially important in a city of "off-the-record" comments; of "background briefings" usually limited to a few chosen reporters or radio and TV correspondents; of "inside sources," "high sources" (especially at the State Department), "anonymous" Senators, and so on. Participants were not even allowed the congressional courtesy of revising their remarks. What was said was said.

An invitation to appear at a Sperling breakfast was a kind of challenge, a test of one's openness and courage. What came out was usually on the positive side. Things that should have been put on the public record were placed there. Politicians who might otherwise have remained "anonymous sources" became known. The timid became brave; the hesitant and apologetic, outspoken. Why? it must be asked.

I think there were at least five conditions bearing on what happened:

1. The sponsorship of the *Christian Science Monitor*, a publication generally considered in Washington to be restrained; above partisanship at best and bipartisan at worst; objective and fair; and of limited circulation.

2. The character of Godfrey Sperling, who has about him an air of innocence not noticeable in most Washington reporters and newsmen. He seems kindly, certainly disarming, and asks hard questions as though the difficult answer he expects would hurt him as much as the person expected to answer.

3. The hour of the meeting, eight o'clock in the morning, before Washington is well awake, a time of privileged conversation.

4. The room in which the breakfast meetings were generally held. A room of great austerity, monastic in its simplicity and without either political or religious pictures or symbols. Asceticism was the ambience and the decor.

5. The food service, an unchanging menu. Those who accepted an invitation knew what to expect. There were the waiting orange and grapefruit juices and coffee, set out early enough so that by the time the guests arrived, both had reached room temperature, or very near. The first course, usually cantaloupe or a fruit compote; the eggs, which followed, complemented by bacon and fried potatoes of unusual shape and consistency, the whole complex— eggs, bacon, and potatoes—served at a temperature slightly above that of the human body.

All of these forces, personalities, institutions, general environment,and food came together so that for the running of one hour at least, even the dishonest were moved to truthfulness.

MORE OF

THE WALL STREET JOURNAL

IS ACTUALLY LESS

(*Culpeper News*, DECEMBER 3, 1981)

The Wall Street Journal, for nearly a century a journal of financial and trade information, in 1981 was enlarged in both format and scope.

In the earlier *Journal*, all was included between a front and a back page made out of one sheet of paper and folded around the interior contents. The paper was a convenient size; it could be folded in a briefcase or carried easily on display under the arm of a junior executive on his way to the subway or to the Eastern shuttle.

The contents were restricted to business and finance, with limited forays into politics, all included in one column, usually limited to 100 to 150 words per item, about the same number of words allowed for the presentation of a crisis on the evening network news.

Then came the expansion, never satisfactorily explained—at least not to me. There were hints from the publishers that they could not resist the possibility of larger advertising revenues to be gained from the expanded edition; that there was internal pressure from the competent staff of the paper for more recognition in print; and that the paper might serve a larger purpose.

The *Journal* now is published in two sections, with a total of about fifty pages. The amount of space given to advertising has greatly increased. A recent issue contained, in addition to the traditional advertisements, ads for automobiles and motorcycles, and a full-page ad for the *New York Times*. In it, the *Times*, with becoming modesty, described itself as the embodiment of "integrity" and as "a symbol" of excellence.

It is not either the quality or quantity of the advertisements that distinguishes the enlarged *Journal* from the former simpler and smaller publication, as much as it is the new and different news stories, special items, and features. For example, one issue carried a long story reporting that an open-pit miner in Silver City, Nevada, preferred working above ground in the open-pit operation to working in an underground mine. Among the reasons for his preference: above ground, one could see the sunsets, and also, if the miner was as sensitive as the author of the *Journal* piece, "a nearby canyon wall, soaked by the soft rays," which "look like a chiseled mound of marmalade."

"A chiseled mound of marmalade" is a little bit hard to imagine or envision at any time or place, but especially when one comes on it, quite by accident, while looking through *The Wall Street Journal* for stock market reports, projections of long- and short-term interest rates, and the like.

The same edition also carried a long report on the state of British politics, described as the "capsule view that emerges, with varying shades of emphasis and assorted hedges," and a reflective piece on the partial shutdown of the federal government because of the budget dispute between President Reagan and the Congress. Congress and the presidential office have in other administrations come very close to comparable showdowns and shutdowns. The consequences have never been very serious; nor were they in this case. The disruption of government services fell short of that which occurs when government employees are sent home early in Washington because of unexpected snowstorms. The *Journal* nodded approvingly over the orderly anticipation of the prospective shutdown by government agencies, but then went on to the heavy observation that "this behavior stood in some real contrast to the incoherence that the brief budget crisis revealed in the larger political process."

It is difficult again to imagine just what "incoherence in the process" is. But the author helped clear things up by saying that although "many of us have done a fair amount of screaming at the arrogant federal bureaucrats for abusing their great discretion and for loading their personal political agendas on the backs of their fellow citizens, . . . a moment like this one reminds us how often their excesses are at bottom the signs of their political masters' eagerness to hide behind complexity . . . etc." These same masters also suffer "from a failure of responsibility." Somewhere amid all of this, and additional articles on U.S.-USSR arms negotiations, past and prospective, and a report that Polish soldiers were being sent back into the provinces, I found that the Budget Crisis had not had any measurable effect on the market.

I am of the opinion that the *Journal* served both appearances and realities better in its earlier short format.

THE PRESS AND POLITICS

(1988)

Thomas Babington Macaulay, nineteenth-century English statesman, historian, and essayist, observed that there was nothing so
ridiculous as the English people engaged in one of their periodic
bouts of self-criticism, remorse, and moral reform. Macaulay had
never seen the American press, or elements of the media, engaged
in similar acts of self-examination, apology, or defense, with accompanying resolutions of reform and purification.

The media are especially prone to such inquiry in campaign years.
In 1988 the first such self-examination centered on the question of
whether the press, and other media, had gone too far in searching

out and reporting moral faults and failings on the part of presidential candidates, especially in the case of Gary Hart. Their conclusion was that they had not gone too far, but that events, facts, and realities had forced the media to provide coverage. Reporting of personal faults did not stop with the Hart case.

The defenses, generally, are comparable to those made by Al Friendly of the *Washington Post*, who attempted to explain and excuse the press for its part in building up and sustaining the anti-Communist and cold war attitudes of the fifties, even though he acknowledged that within a month after Senator Joseph McCarthy's famous Wheeling, West Virginia, speech in February of 1950, it was clear that he was using fraudulent material. Why did the press act as it did? Because, said Friendly, "at the outset, for the first week or so, and before they could be examined, McCarthy's charges appeared to be of the most profound national security significance and might, quite possibly, be true."

Then, he said, the Senate panicked and held hearings. "For the press to have ignored the most newsworthy event in the Congress (however phony the thing was beginning to look), the focus of congressional and, almost at once, national attention, is preposterous." The fact is that it was press coverage that made the charges the matter of "profound national" attention. And it was the press coverage of the Senate hearings that made those hearings significant.

Again the press failed miserably in covering the Vietnam War. Long after there was massive evidence that members of the administration, especially Dean Rusk and Robert McNamara, did not know what they were talking about in stating military needs, in describing events in Vietnam, and in projecting victory, the press dutifully headlined their every statement, and printed facts from administration handouts, almost without challenge or question. Most newspapers and the other media generally continued to support the war well into 1969, despite realization as to what the situation was and what was happening in Vietnam. The most telling evidence of this failure was the *New York Times*'s publication of the events at the

My Lai number-four hamlet, Song My village, in March of 1968, where, according to the *Times*, "American troops caught a North Vietnamese force in a pincer movement on the central coastal plain yesterday, killing 128 enemy soldiers in day-long fighting. . . .

"While the two companies of United States Marines moved in on the enemy force from opposite sides, heavy artillery barrages and armed helicopters were called in to pound the North Vietnamese soldiers. . . ." This dramatic operation, it was later determined, was in fact the My Lai Massacre.

The media's behavior during the Vietnam War, as in the McCarthy period, proved the observation that the press acts like blackbirds in the fall, settled on a telephone wire. When one flies away, all fly away. When one returns, all return.

Most of the media appeared not to have discovered the truth about the Vietnam War until after publication of the *Pentagon Papers*, which was widely called a heroic act, performed in the name of freedom of the press—that is, by the press. There was little that was surprising in the *Papers*. To discover that persons in the Pentagon had actually talked about the war and raised questions about operations, tactics, even purposes, should not have been surprising. That there were plans to stifle criticism, and that the whole truth was not being told to Congress, the press, or the American people was not news to anyone who followed that war closely, as the press should have.

As the '88 election campaign progresses, the media will occasionally question their methods and their substantive reporting, but one can be certain they will not find themselves seriously deficient or wanting. The media are demonstrating the truth of an observation by Oswald Spengler that there are never but two estates operating in a society, the civil and the religious. When one formerly recognized loses power, that power is picked up by the other, in some form. Whereas churches often question the infallibility of church spokesmen and leaders, editors continue to publish, claiming that their power and authority can be traced to unsigned editorials (some back to Moses, who came down from the mountain with the first unsigned editorial). Columnists, TV commentators, and anchormen stop just short of claiming the clerical power and insights once covered and sustained by "grace of office."

More limited and pragmatic powers have also been picked up by the press. The press has its own index, determining what the public should read or hear or see. The ultimate expression of this power is in the *New York Times*'s masthead, which asserts that the *Times* prints "All the news that's fit to print." One can fairly ask, by whose determination? The media run a kind of beautification and canonization procedure, and also determine who is to be forgotten, if not censored, and condemned.

Protecting one's sources is a secular application of the religious principle of the "seal of the confessional," as is the practice of not exposing the faults and failures of news and media persons, on the grounds that such exposure might denigrate or reduce confidence in the media.

Both of these principles were applied by the *New York Times* in its report of a marijuana party given by Dr. Bourne, Jimmy Carter's drug advisor. The first report was carried in the *Times*. The paper stated its source as two *Times* reporters, or employees, who attended the party as invited guests. The story was not reported by either or both, but by another *Times* reporter to whom they told the story. The reporter who made the story public refused to reveal the source, protecting those who had confessed. The *Times* subsequently defended its suppression of the names of the sources and participants in the party by saying it would not publish information that might reflect adversely on the press, tend to discredit it, and cause people to lose confidence in it.

Do not worry. The process can do no harm, and very little good. The conclusion will be that the press, under difficult circumstances, has done as well as or better than could have been expected. The media will survive and are not likely to be worse for the exercise. The situation is similar to what happens when monkeys at the zoo get involved with examining each other or themselves. The work is serious. There is a great deal of scratching and scrutiny. Something is usually found, or appears to be found. Sometimes it is merely tasted, sometimes it is eaten after careful consideration, sometimes it is shared with the others. In the end, the monkeys appear to be deeply satisfied. Life in the zoo goes on as before.

KEEPING THE AIRWAVES

SPOTLESSLY CLEAN

(1986)

I note that there is a movement—inspired, it seems, principally by wives of members of Congress—to set up a rating or censorship procedure for rock music. There are, it seems, bad words and thoughts beneath or amid all the noise and shouting that make up rock. The proposal is that a warning be put on the record or tape, something like that on cigarette packages and comparable to the rating system used for movies. Just what the code will be has not yet been made public.

If the proposal carries, I anticipate that warnings will have to be given during broadcasts of rock programs, and on regular radio programs, advising that the sound should be turned down for an up-coming record if there are persons under twenty-one, or under sixteen, or under ten in the room. Young audiences would be advised that they may listen to the record if their parents are present and ready to give explanations and guidance, as they are supposed to do about some movies.

I don't have very strong feelings about this rating system. Nor do I feel that it will have much effect on those who are attracted to rock music. Television has long carried warnings about programs about to be presented. The television warnings advise that forthcoming scenes may be too much for young eyes and minds. Some are. But I have yet to see a warning for children and adults to beware of advertisements about to be shown—that they are vulgar, obscene, or show disrespect.

I was struck by this after watching Dan Rather showing great compassion for the victims of the earthquake in Mexico City and finishing the evening news with a deeply religious reflection on the meaning of life and death in Mexico City. His reflection was preceded by an advertisement for hemorrhoidal relief, and was followed immediately by an advertisement featuring a man in a Roman collar, presumably a priest, demonstrating the virtues of Polident for cleaning and whitening false teeth.

Here, too, as in the case of the rating system for rock-music warnings, I have no certain position. But if we are going to get into warnings and admonitions of what can and cannot be watched or heard safely, I have an opinion. I would place first importance on advance warnings that some programs to be presented should not be watched by policemen or law-enforcement officers.

I suspect that the aerial bombing of the MOVE group in Philadelphia may have been encouraged by police officers watching television lawmen using helicopters in their protective maneuvers. Patrolmen in automobiles certainly must be encouraged to reckless pursuit by watching the almost-nightly automobile chases through the streets of major cities, and possibly are encouraged to shoot by the quick and ready use of guns by both male and female television police officers.

Other programs might depress policemen, or detectives, who are presented as relatively, if not absolutely, stupid, and regularly saved from folly by the brilliance of private detectives.

It follows, then, that doctors should be warned against shows such as "General Hospital," and lawyers against "People's Court." Since I no longer have small children at home, I have concentrated my efforts on my dog, Molly, whom I have banned from watching a Saturday morning program called "Scoobie-Doo," which features a dog that could potentially encourage vices, such as cowardice and gluttony, in canine viewers.

CRISIS WATCH:

THE RATCHET OF READINESS

(1981)

"This is Dan Rather on 'Crisis Watch'. You may be surprised to find me, us, on watch when there is no visible, identified crisis."

"The Three Mile Island reactor is under control, it seems. There is no report of new or impending activity at Mount Saint Helen's. Afghanistan is no longer considered a crisis by the press. I am not there, as you know. And Zbig Brzezinski is not standing guard at the Khyber Pass. Poland has been taken off the critical list. Energy supplies are increasing relative to demand, and prices are going down. The Iranian hostages are back. The crisis countdown, or countup, has ended. The space shuttle is back. The tiles, which we repeatedly warned you might come off when the craft re-entered the earth's heavy atmosphere, did not come off. The president is back at work following the attempt on his life. The pope is recovering. And the changing of the anchorman on the evening news here at CBS, the passing of the microphone and teleprompter from Walter Cronkite to me, has passed the critical point.

"You might well ask, 'Why the crisis watch?' That is a fair question. It deserves an answer. The answer is, 'Because everything is too quiet.' The rule for a good newsman is 'Never let down.' Be, as the battery advertisement recommends, 'Ever-ready.' The camera not only 'never blinks,' it 'never sleeps.'

"Because of the ominous quiet, we have deployed our ace correspondents to major crisis points, or potential crisis points.

"Nelson Benton, who has been tested under fire in Vietnam, has been sent to the quietest, possibly the most dangerous place, therefore, Philadelphia. He is watching Independence Hall, the cradle of our liberty.

"Nelson, are you there?"

"Right here, Dan."

"Is it quiet in Philadelphia, Nelson?"

"Very quiet, Dan."

"What of the report that termites are in the timbers of the hall? I know that it is hard to get a picture of termites in action, but can you get them on sound? Can we hear them moving or eating?"

"Officials here, Dan, are monitoring the timbers regularly. They say that there is no sound of termite action. We have applied our own sound technology, and our findings sustain the silence findings of the local authorities."

"Nelson, is it safe to say that Independence Hall for the time being is safe and solid, and that the termite action, discovered recently, has been arrested?"

"Yes, Dan."

"Thank you, Nelson.

"And now to the State Department, of which, I believe Secretary

Alexander Haig said, 'The crisis starts here,' and Diane Sawyer. Diane, your hair looks lovely. Oh, I'm sorry. Our crisis watch was interrupted by a commercial. That was not Diane but an advertisement for Breck shampoo. There you are, Diane. Is there any sign of an emerging crisis at the State Department? Before you answer me, would you explain to our viewers the difference between a high source of information and a higher source of information at the State Department?"

"Yes, Dan, here at the State Department building there are seven floors. High sources are on the sixth floor as a rule, although under pressure, we State Department correspondents may call a fifth-floor source a 'high source.' Higher sources are all on the seventh floor. There is no report of any crisis from any level today, Dan, and no rumor that a crisis has been quelled or quashed."

"Thank you, Diane, and now would you move a little to the right? I want to point out to our viewers and listeners the spot, actually more than a spot, a country, a new country, Belize, in Central America, which may become a crisis point. It seems calm on the map today.

"And now to check the conditions of our gold reserves at Fort Knox. These reserves have not been checked officially, according to my information, since Secretary of the Treasury George Humphrey, in the Eisenhower administration, checked them and found that we had approximately one ounce more than was recorded. George Herman, our economic reporter, is on guard at Fort Knox. George, the dollar, according to reports from the London Gold Exchange, is falling against gold. Have you noticed any unusual activity at the fort? Brink's trucks, coming and going, for example?"

"No, Dan. No Brink's trucks, but one air-conditioning truck has been admitted through the security gate. The word we have is that an air-conditioning unit in one of the gold-storage areas has broken down. There is no immediate problem. However, gold experts tell me that if the air-conditioner is not repaired, in fifty to one hundred years measurable oxidation of the gold reserve will take place, and the gold will be debased through oxidation, which might add as much as four or five ounces in weight to the reserves. There is no immediate crisis at Fort Knox, Dan. We will stand by and report to you as soon as the air-conditioner is fixed."

"Thank you very much, George. That report should be reassuring to the money markets of the world.

"And now to Ike Pappas, who is standing by, possibly sitting by, at the Pentagon. Ike, what is the crisis reading at the Pentagon?"

"Dan, I am here at the angle between side one and side two of the Pentagon. All seems calm on these two sides. The problem at the Pentagon is that one can never see more than two sides at a time, leaving three sides unwatched. A triangular design would have been better."

"That is very perceptive, Ike, but could you tell me what, if any, has been the effect of the new order that the military personnel at the Pentagon wear uniforms, four out of five working days. Has this changed morale? What has been the reaction in the Soviet Union, where, I am informed, the military personnel operate in full force, and in uniform, six days a week? Has there been any Russian reaction, that you know of, to the new uniform order here? Would you say that 'the ratchet of readiness' has been advanced a notch as a result of the order?"

"Dan, I do not have a definitive answer to any one of your questions, but I do have one important observation to make. There is an air of elation here at the Pentagon over President Reagan's decision to revive and rebuild the cavalry. Intelligence has known for a long time that the Soviets have been building up their cavalry under cover, although they claim that the horses and riders would be used only in making movies. It is now estimated that the Russians have at least three thousand cavalry horses and men. The United States, officially, has only twenty-eight or twenty-nine horses in our military establishment. They are kept at Fort Myer, near Washington, and are used only for military funerals. You may have seen one team used in the recent burial ceremony of General Omar Bradley. Inner sources here at the Pentagon—we do not have higher sources at the Pentagon, as the correspondents at the State Department have, but peripheral, inner, and innermost sources—say that closing the cavalry gap is the top priority in Pentagon plans. Orders will soon go out for the registration of all quarter horses. American saddlebreds, Morgans, and Arabians. Opposition from the Humane Society is expected to be marginal. The hope is that enough horses, especially Arabians, for possible use in the Middle East, will volunteer, or be volunteered. If not, it is likely a draft of horses between the ages of five and eight years will be considered essential. There is no plan to register or draft Thoroughbreds at this time."

"Thank you very much, Ike, for that reassuring report. 'For want of a nail the shoe was lost; for want of a shoe the horse was lost; and for want of a horse the rider was lost.' This report on the prospective cavalry buildup is a first for CBS, is it not, Ike?

"And now to Lesley Stahl at the White House, the penultimate stop in our crisis check. It is at the White House, that Harry Truman, as I recall, said, 'The crisis stops here.' There you are, Lesley, right there among the holly bushes. Everything looks calm there on the White House lawn. The weather must be mild, Lesley. I note that you are wearing a cotton print, rather than one of your late spring suits with scarf."

"Yes, Dan, everything is calm here."

"Lesley, may I interrupt? What is that hanging from the branch of the elm tree above your head? Could it be a crisis?"

"No, it's Sam Donaldson of ABC."

"Is he trying to bite you in the neck? You know his reputation."

"No, no. Dan, this is Sam. Lesley wouldn't give me my turn in the holly bushes. This is the only way I could get on camera to do my evening stand-up, or should I say 'hang-down.' You can run me upside down as a crisis on CBS if you want to. I will appear on ABC, however, as though kneeling, with a log across the back of my legs. My hair will appear to be standing on end, when in fact it will be hanging on end."

"Dan, this is Lesley. Everything is fine here. Sam has just fallen out of the tree during the commercial and is lying in the holly bushes behind me. He is not seriously hurt. There is no crisis at the White House. Secretary Haig is not here."

"Thank you, Lesley, for standing firm and reporting under difficult circumstances.

"And now to our ultimate crisis checkpoint and Lem Tucker. Lem, as you know, was the correspondent on the spot during the recent assassination attempt on President Reagan. Lem, are you there?"

"Yes, Dan, I am."

"Where are you, Lem?"

"Dan, I don't know where I am. Somewhere between a stakeout on Janet Cooke, former *Washington Post* reporter and temporary holder of the Pulitzer Prize for creative journalism, and the panda pen at the National Zoo. It is very dark here, Dan. We have lost our lights. I cannot see my hands before my face. I think we are under the Taft Bridge."

"Good, Lem, a critical point, a favorite site for suicides in Washington. Keep the cameras running."

"I will, Dan, until we run out of tape."

"Good for you, Lem.

"Well, that just about wraps up our crisis coverage for today. You will excuse me, I am having Bob Schieffer, who has been standing by, take over from me. I am going to check on the whereabouts of Walter Cronkite. I do that regularly. You may recall that during the crisis surrounding the attempt on the life of President Reagan, we lost contact with Walter. He was, according to a report, sailing in his sloop, or ketch, on Long Island Sound at the time. Walter is, as you know, now covering 'the Universe,' for CBS. It is an ambitious program and requires much travel to distant and strange places, some of it in simulators. Following our loss of contact with Walter during the presidential crisis, we resolved that such a loss would never occur again. A small transmitter, a fallout from the space program, has been implanted in Walter's neck muscle, not unlike those transmitters that are placed in polar bears and wolves so that their movements in the wilderness can be traced. When I am on the air, as I now am, I carry a small black box, which picks up the signal from Walter. Control has just signaled me that we are pick-ing up Walter's signal. He is just leaving China, after failing in his plan to film the giant panda in Sichuan, a freshwater fishery, and the use of Chinese medicinal herbs. Walter is not leaving, as has been reported, in a 'huff,' or in a 'wok'—I mean a walk—or a junk, but by air. Here is Bob.''

ALL PRESIDENTS' DAY

(1987)

All Presidents' Day caught me by surprise. I had not known that all separate presidents' birthdays had been wiped out, homogenized, and consolidated into one day of observance, although I was vaguely aware that Lincoln's birthday had passed without much recognition.

Then, what used to be singularly and particularly and personally George Washington's birthday approached. I noted not only the traditional "white sales," which had been associated with George and Martha, who seemed to be heavily into sheets and pillowcases (possibly, if we accept some doubtful historical data, because of

George's disposition to sleep in so many places), but announcements of "All Presidents' Sales"—sales of all kinds of things, especially of automobiles.

Armistice Day, I knew, had already been made nonhistoric and renamed "Veterans Day." I disapproved of that change, being of the opinion that the end of World War I deserves a day on the annual calendar, as do V-E Day and V-J Day. Memorial Day easily could have been expanded to include all veterans—the dead, the living, and those missing in action. Consolidations like these were probably inevitable following the acceptance of the moving of days from their fixed and proper historical date—if such dates occurred in midweek—to Monday or Friday so as to lengthen the weekend for either commercial or leisure purposes.

They may have been foreshadowed even earlier and in a more subtle way with the introduction of homogenized food products. One of the first such products was homogenized milk. Its cream content did not show in the neck of the bottle and could not be poured off for special use; it was reduced to being reported as a percentage of butterfat not evident to the human eye. Homogenized peanut butter followed. One jar of pre-homogenized peanut butter provided at least three taste experiences. The first came immediately after the jar was opened. At the top of the jar was a layer of oil to be mixed into the more solid contents. In the second stage, the peanut butter tasted much more like modern homogenized peanut butter, but in the last stages of use, what was left in the jar took on a special character—dry and crunchy—somewhat like peanut-butter candy bars or cookies.

Consolidations may have been encouraged by some religious practices. The more liturgical churches have long celebrated All Saints' Day, a catch-up observance designed to pick up those saints who had not been identified or canonized, and to pay attention to those who were recognized but who might not have received enough attention or honor. In a somewhat circumspect and careful action, the church dedicates another day not to "All Popes," but to "All Holy Popes." "All Good Presidents' Day" might do as well.

If the reductionists, the homogenizers, and the consolidators continue to have their way, more and more holidays and days of special observation and note may be changed. Mother's Day, now singular and personal, may be generalized to embrace all mothers, including Ma Barker and Mother Jones. Columbus Day could lose its historical singularity and be renamed "Discoverers' Day," so as not to exclude St. Brendan, the Vikings, and any others who may have passed by.

Pearl Harbor Day could be rechristened "Ship Attack Day," thus encompassing "Remembering the *Maine*," the *Lusitania*, and possibly even the Tonkin Gulf "incident." Christmas could become simply "The Holiday," and everyone's birthday could be celebrated together on "All Birthdays' Day"—say, January 1, the day on which all Thoroughbred racehorses are presumed, for some reason, to have been born.

A SHORT HISTORY

OF THE NEUTRON BOMB

(*Culpeper News*, OCTOBER 1, 1981)

The neutron bomb had a modest beginning in calculations made on the back of an old envelope by S. T. Cohen, known as "the Father of the Neutron Bomb." It has no known or identified "mother." The theory and calculations were soon put to the test of technology and found workable. The essential parts of the bomb were manufactured during the administration of President Jimmy Carter, assembled in the administration of President Ronald Reagan, deployed in the administration of his successor, and used by the subsequent president in the millennial year A.D. 3000. Tests in the 1970s were conducted on monkeys, never on human beings, according to Defense Department officials of the time. Estimates of biological effects of the bomb on human beings were "synthesized."

In the early experiments, monkeys were placed in cubicles called "squeeze boxes" and exposed to radiation doses similar to those that would be released in the explosion of a neutron bomb. The monkeys used in the test had been trained to run on a treadmill.

The radiation, according to the testers, did not pain the monkeys. Five seconds after the exposure, each animal was put back on the treadmill. Results varied from monkey to monkey, but 80 percent became incapacitated within eight minutes of the exposure. All of the monkeys eventually died.

Some scientists then held that the results of exposure found in monkeys could not with certainty be directly translatable to human beings. "Clinical information," they said, would be the only way to determine human reaction.

Later studies under more natural conditions (a contained monkey farm) achieved results more applicable to the human condition. Monkeys exposed to the heavy blast reacted much as did the monkeys in the squeeze box. For those outside the range of heavy dosage, death did not come quickly. There was evidence of discomfort, if not pain, and much vomiting. The monkey house itself was unharmed.

Monkeys at the outer range of the enclosure did not appear to suffer any immediate effects, but succeeding generations of the exposed monkeys began to show mutations. Tails grew shorter, and finally disappeared. The amount of body hair decreased. Forelegs grew shorter. Eventually there was a generation that stood up and walked on its hind legs at about sixteen months of age and began to say words such as "da-da" and "mama."

Some grew up and were trained to be tank operators. In the millennial war of the year 3000, their tanks were targets of the neutron bomb. Those that were in tanks at or near the center of the blast were incapacitated within eight minutes. All of those eventually died, continuing until the last moment to drive the tanks, which, even after the death of their operators, continued to run on until stopped by walls, or rivers, or lack of fuel. Operators outside the central area of the blast died more slowly. They showed evidence of discomfort, if not pain, and vomited profusely.

Others, farther removed from the blast area, did not appear to suffer any immediate effects, but succeeding generations began to show mutations. They began to grow tails. The amount of body hair increased. Their arms began to grow longer. They stooped more, and eventually began to walk on four feet, to speak a different language, and to spend more and more time in trees. They had a strong attachment to treadmills.

OF TIME AND TELEVISION

(1987)

Time is not easy to handle; it is tough and evasive. It has baffled philosophers. Aristotle's best effort was to say that time is not "itself movement but neither does time exist without change. Time is neither movement, nor independent of movement." Moreover, although he held that a continuous quantity is divisible, time, "past, present, and future, forms a continuous whole." Time, he said, seems to be an "indivisible instant."

Theologians have been less troubled by time than have philosophers. Theologians accept time essentially on faith, holding that since God created the world, He must have created time, or that time came with creation, and therefore was concomitant to the act. "There is no time before the world," asserted St. Augustine, writing as a theologian, not a philosopher. He said that what we call the present has "no extent or duration," and that only past or future time could be long or short. Past and future have duration, he held, but then he asked, "In what sense can that which does not exist be long or short? The past no longer is; the future is not yet." This theory was challenged by George Allen, the longtime successful coach of the Washington Redskins, who in his player selection and game strategy followed the principle "The future is now."

Theologians seem less interested in the beginning of time than are philosophers, and are more concerned about the manner and the time of its ending, and with what comes after that. St. Thomas Aquinas held that time existed in God or with Him, although time was not particularly important until after the creation of the world and the division of the work into seven days, or periods. St. Thomas tried to sort out time by defining two "nows": the "eternal now" and the "first, or beginning, now," from which our time begins.

Politicians, especially in presidential elections, play fast and loose with concepts of time. In the 1984 campaign, for example, there were assertions that one party or the other in power would "recapture our destiny," which has obviously not yet been captured, and also "reshape our future," which has not yet been shaped.

God, insofar as the record can be traced, did not meddle much with time once it began. He did stop the sun in the heavens, a kind of first daylight-saving time, to help Joshua finish the Battle of Jericho, but He did not lengthen the day, only the time of light. Politicians have done the same with modern daylight-saving time, although some critics have charged them with meddling with God's time, and dairy farmers have protested that the change has affected the flow of milk from their cows.

Poets have been less passive and reflective in dealing with time than have the theologians and philosophers. They have resented it, denounced it, challenged it, ignored it, or made the best of it.

Shakespeare, the master, played the whole range of relationships. He surrendered to it in one sonnet:

> Ruin hath taught me thus to ruminate
> That time will come and take my love away.

In another sonnet, he struck back in challenge:

> Do thy worst, Old Time, despite thy wrong
> My love shall in my verse ever live young.

John Milton seemed to be afraid to challenge time, asserting that he would in eternity get even:

> And glut thyself with what thy womb devours,
> Which is no more than what is false and vain,
> And merely mortal dross;
> So little is our loss
> So little is thy gain.
> For when as each thing bad thou hast entomb'd,
> And last of all thy greedy self consum'd,
> Then long Eternity shall greet our bliss
> With an individual kiss. . . .
> Then all this earthly grossness quit,
> Attir'd with stars, we shall for ever sit,
> Triumphing over Death, and Chance, and thee,
> O Time.

Lesser poets have been more ready to compromise, suggesting that we make the best, or most, of time. One wrote:

> Be a gleaner of time
> Claim what runs through the hour glass
> When no one watches
> What is counted by clocks, ticking
> When no one listens
> Save remnants

From the cutting room of day
End pieces from the loom of night
Brand and hold
Unmarked, maverick minutes
Salvage time left derelict
By those who despair of light
Yet fear the dark
Steal only from sleep
And from eternity
Of which time no one dares ask
What? or Where?

The general historical record is that people have been and are rather accepting of time, not attempting to either understand or control it. They try to get along with it, occasionally hanging an adjective on it in passing, or subjecting it to a verb of some usefulness. Most of the adjectives are uncomplimentary: "devouring," "bloody," "avenging," "threatening," "demanding," "deceiving," "relentless," "greedy"; or obvious, like "past and present," "early and late," "good and bad." The words applied have been quite direct, like the adjectives. Thus, time is "wasted" and "saved"; it is "lost" and "found"; it has been "released" and "regained"; it is "served." Time is occasionally "taken out," and then "declared" in again; there is "free time" and "borrowed time."

The time measurers took a wholly different approach. They abandoned hope of understanding time, and undertook to measure and control it. "Try anything" was their theory, so they tried drops of water, sand in an hourglass, notched wheels with weights moved by springs, electric impulses, ions. The appearance, if not the reality, of controlling time was found marketable in every society. In today's backward societies, along with an English bicycle or an American ballpoint pen, a watch—preferably Swiss, though Japanese makes will do—is a sure mark of status, even of upward mobility. As in more advanced civilizations, the wearer can at least appear to have some mastery over time. He can set his watch backward or forward. He can look at the dial as though he were supposed to be where he is, or possibly to indicate he should be somewhere else, or must go there soon.

Immediacy became a factor with the introduction of the wristwatch, eliminating the delay that went with the use of the pocket watch, especially the kind that had a protective cover. In early modern civilization, roughly 1950 to 1975, watchmakers attacked time most subtly. They introduced the self-winding watch to free the busy man or woman from the primitive task of winding. Newer watches drew their power from more mysterious, scientific, non-human sources. Ions were "in."

At the same time as the power sources of watches were changing, so was the face of the watch. The lower classes and less important persons might have a watch with hours, minutes, and even seconds indicated, but the movers and shakers, and those aspiring to such status, budgeted their time in larger lots. The second hand was the first to go. Numerals began to disappear, until, in some cases, only four markers divided the day and the night into quarters. Then followed watches with no numerals or markers. Finally, the "in" thing for super, *super* executives, was to wear no watch at all, thus defying time itself, and possibly even death along with it. In so doing, they give a partial response to philosophers, as though to say, "I will measure the now by my changing, and my changing by the now," and to the theologians, "I shall measure as I am measured."

Along with radio and television came a new treatment of time. Time was offered for sale, and, as a result, necessarily graded. Old categories were cast aside; time was rated as "prime," "choice," and "good"—the same grade designations, incidentally, used in the evaluation of beef, with three additional classes at the lower level of quality.

Treatment of time on radio and television is not limited to commercial application. These same media have attacked the philosophical and theological conceptions of time as well. Whereas most philosophers hold, or have held, that no moment of time is like any other moment, radio and television mavens say that there is such a thing as equal time. Whereas philosophers say that every moment of time is unlike every other moment of time, except for the incidentals that pass through it, radio and television say, without concern for contradiction, that there is "unique time," not equal to or like any other time. Thus they identify "Maude" 's time, Cronkite's time, "Kojak" 's time, marked forever. Radio and television have also introduced other conceptions of time, such as "shared time," "pooled time," and "time slots," and have asserted control over time that had been denied to God by theologians—at least until the world ends. Thus television interviewers, without apology to God or the theologians, regularly say, "We [or you] are out of time."

AN ALTERNATIVE
TO MAKING LIFE A CRIME

(Washington Star, SEPTEMBER 18, 1977)

America is fast becoming a felonious society. The old saying that "there ought to be a law against it" scarcely applies today since almost everything that can be made the object of a law has been covered. And under new federal election laws, it has become increasingly risky to run for office for fear of violating the criminal code.

Citizens who would petition the government, especially in an organized way, are threatened by new lobbying bills with possible criminal penalties. Some businessmen operate within the range of criminal prosecution. Citizens who attempt to fill out their own tax returns are in danger.

A recent report of enlistments in the armed services states that more than 22,000 enlistees concealed criminal records, which made them subject to a $10,000 fine and to imprisonment. (The military, in this case exercising commendable restraint, kept two out of three of those who concealed criminal records, and prosecuted no one.)

Even legal betting involves relatively high risk. Nonbettors know that the only winner in the long run, and often in the short run, is the tack or the house—or the government that collects its cut on each bet. As of May 1, federal tax law required tracks to withhold 20 percent of any win over $1,000. Andrew Beyer, the track and betting expert of the *Washington Star*, is correct in stating that those who bet on the horses and participate in other forms of legal gambling are treated worse than any other persons subject to the Internal Revenue Code. They usually find, he writes, that it is impossible to prove their losses to the satisfaction of the IRS. They cannot carry losses forward. They are allowed no deductible expenses. Certainly the cost of collecting taxes on gambling earnings bears no relationship to what is collected.

Attitudes toward crime and punishment and toward gambling are different in Australia. In the course of my ten-day visit to that country recently, there were at least two news stories reflecting this difference.

The first story involved the secretary-manager of the Fitzroy Football Club, who was convicted of stealing more than $11,000 from the club's treasury. The defense lawyer pointed out that his client had lost most of his savings in 1974, when he loaned to a close friend a large sum of money that was not repaid. It was also acknowledged that gambling was involved. In view of all the circumstances (including the fact that restitution had been made), the club committee had passed a unanimous resolution recommending that no charges be pressed against the former secretary-manager. He was fined $1,000 and released on a three-year good-behavior bond. It was difficult, the judge said, to sentence a man who devoted his whole life to the community and to football, with little or no reward.

The second story involved Reverend Frank Mulcahy of St. Mary's Roman Catholic Church, Grafton, New South Wales. There is a track at Grafton, and an annual race known as the Grafton Cup. Father Mulcahy included a tip on the race in his weekly parish bulletin. He did not give the name of the horse but drew a cartoon of a horse leaning across a fence and smelling flowers, with a caption reading, "How sweet it is. Good punting."

The faithful got the message, which was a bet on a horse named Sweet Aroma. The mare won at 36-to-1 odds. St. Mary's parishioners were such big winners that the track did not have enough money on hand to pay them off, and a bank was opened to provide the funds.

If the same had happened in the United States, Father Mulcahy probably would have been arraigned before a diocesan council for discipline. He might have been found in violation of state or federal law for encouraging gambling or giving suggested odds without a license. And the IRS probably would have been waiting at his church the next Sunday, demanding 20 percent of the collection.

ON THE DECLINE

OF SPY STANDARDS

(1987)

The rash of spies, informers, defectors, and other varieties of trai-
tors who have been publicly exposed in recent weeks and months
is, if judged by the classical standards by which operators in this
field have traditionally been judged, a rather common and motley
lot. There are the slight exceptions of Larry Wu-tai Chin and the
Soviet lover of Vitaly Yurchenko, who bear marks of distinction—
Chin because his reticence and strong loyalty to the Chinese lend
a touch of class to his drama, and the latter because her sense of
honor and propriety led her to the most dramatic of all forms of
expression, suicide.

In the period surrounding World War II, there were standards to which spies, informers, and defectors conformed. If the espionage involved a first-class power such as the United States, the spy would be expected to be moved by high ideological motives such as a desire for universal and perpetual peace, or, on the negative side, saving the world through mutually assured destruction, thus not letting one side or the other get a destruction advantage.

Russians who defected during this period usually gave a more limited ideological justification, and were more likely to make their case one of personal rejection of life in the Soviet Union, and of the restrictions placed on their artistic expression. This was especially true of ballet dancers and musicians, and an occasional poet. Russians did not defect in order to play hockey, or soccer, or to join the international ski circuit. Such defections were more likely among lesser Communist and Communist satellite nations.

The motivations of British spies and informers were usually, or certainly very often, found to involve homosexual relationships. These relationships seemed to move the persons involved to rise above patriotic restraints.

Third-class countries might produce spies moved by the more acceptable sexual attractions in the heterosexual order, while spies and informers from fourth-class countries were moved by crass financial and materialistic considerations. The old standards no longer hold.

Russians now defect for material considerations, even for money, which may not be paid to them by a government directly, but realized through advances and royalties on books and what they may be paid by the news media for public appearances. Defectors, like hostages or former hostages, are quickly sought out by agents.

Homosexuality, having become more accepted, has lost its distinction and power in the world of international intrigue. The disease AIDS may even drive it completely out of international affairs. Regular sex seems to continue to be effective, as in the case of the recent Soviet defector, Mr. Yurchenko, who eventually redefected. All of his turnings seemed to come to naught when the woman, a

Russian, asserted (before her suicide) that she had been loved "by a spy, not a defector." Love, too, seems to have been involved to a degree in the case of an American woman who passed information to her Ghanaian lover, and also in the case of Richard Miller, an FBI agent who is reported to have mixed sex and money in selling counterintelligence to a Soviet woman with whom he was having an affair.

Other American spies whose behavior has been exposed seem to have been motivated by what had been classically reserved for citizens of fourth-class countries, that is, money or material goods.

The Walker clan seems to have been above or indifferent to ideological considerations, and looked only to the bottom line. Ronald Pelton, former communications specialist for the National Security Agency, evidently sold information to the Soviet Union without an ideological motivation; and Jonathan Jay Pollard, along with his wife, both linked to espionage for Israel, seem to be spies for hire.

The Pollard model suggests that spies may soon offer themselves, or be offered, by service companies. They may soon sell their services like Pinkerton or Fingerhut agents, and we will become accustomed to spy agencies, just as we have detective agencies, which will, in turn, be quickly represented by television series that depict the topsy-turvy, dangerous, but devil-may-care lifestyles of international spies-for-hire, in the domestic television manner of "A-Team," "Simon & Simon," or "The Equalizer."

AT THE MOMENT

OF A POET'S DEATH,

STAND UP AND BE QUIET

(Washington Star, SEPTEMBER 18, 1977)

When a king dies, the popular cry is, "The King is dead. Long live the King." When a poet dies, there should be quiet. The life of a poet and his works are seldom well served by the canned obituaries released on the day of death. Just as the deaths of most politicians, including kings, are predictable, so are their obituaries. Not so with poets. Poets should not be too quickly honored in death, as politicians usually are, especially by those who failed to honor them in life.

Robert Lowell was recognized as the preeminent American poet of our time, and was honored as he deserved, within the range of the honor and recognition given poets in our culture. He was pleased with the honor and recognition that he received. His complaints, mild as they were, were not personal. They related to the general lot of poets and to what they had to say, not as social or political spokesmen or reformers, but as gifted persons called to witness, understanding and speaking or writing the word.

In discussing criticism of one of his later collections of poetry, he accepted the possible validity of that criticism, except for the suggestion that he had been careless or superficial. He said, "I have thought about every word in the whole collection." Noting one word, the adverb *coldly*, which he used in one poem, he said that he had used it only after a half-day's reflection.

Before the antiwar campaign of 1967–68, I knew Robert Lowell only through his writings and through friends of mine, such as the poet Allen Tate, who knew Lowell.

Robert Lowell came to the antiwar movement (it might be better to say that the movement came to him, for he was an opponent of the war before there was a movement) not as a political activist, or as one wishing to give political advice and counsel, not as one wishing to write political tracts or speeches. Rather, he was there as one who thought that he should be present to witness, even experience, "physical danger," as he did during a protest in a march on the Pentagon, and at a Columbia University demonstration, and as he did in Chicago in the summer of 1968.

In a poem published in 1967, "Waking Early Sunday Morning," Lowell set the tone of the war years with these lines:

O to break loose, All life's grandeur
is something with a girl in summer,
elated as the President
girdled by his establishment.
This Sunday morning, free to chaff
his own thoughts with his bear-cuffed staff,
swimming nude, unbuttoned, sick
of his ghost-written rhetoric.

No week-ends for the gods now. Wars
flicker, earth licks its open sores,
fresh breakage, fresh promotions chance
assassinations, no advance.

Only man thinning out his kind
sounds through the Sabbath noon, the blind
swipe of the pruner and his knife
busy the pruner and his knife
busy about the tree of life.

Robert Lowell followed the election campaign of 1968 through the shoe factories and knitting mills of New Hampshire. He upset the manager of a sweater factory, who considered himself a most enlightened employer, by observing that workers making shoes seemed to be much happier than those who were knitting sweaters. He went to bowling alleys and to baseball parks, and he irritated staff by talking to the candidate for an hour about the origin of the word *fungo*—while the press waited. He flew in small planes over the tamarack swamps and lakes of Wisconsin, still gray with April ice, to be introduced to small inland college audiences as "the poet."

The war saddened Robert Lowell; it did not surprise him. It was another burden on him as he carried on his vocation as a poet, dedicated to understanding life and history. One of his first collections of poetry was appropriately called *Life Studies*. One of his last was called *History*.

While writing this memorial, I received a poem dedicated to Robert Lowell, written after his death. It is entitled "The Nail of the Index Finger" (for Robert Lowell):

In a Washington of poetry reading
and peace marching,
we cruised the lit monuments.
"Jefferson" you said

and filled the space of the dark
with a joke.
"Lincoln" you said,
and quoted the Greeks.

In a small bar
You pulled the bound galleys of "Notebooks,"
out of your pocket.
"Do you like this change?" you asked.
"Do you understand?"

When we said good night
you took my hand
and observed it for a long time
as if it were a visitor from a strange country.
And still holding mine
you pointed to the nail
of your index finger.
"This too will die," you said,
"Imagine, this too will die."

In the sunshine of the next day
we walked up capitol hill
to lunch with your old friend, my new friend,
You gave him the bound galleys
The three of us laughed.
But during the meal, I grew silent,
feeling, for the first time in years,
like a little girl in the company of grown-ups
who will never die.

Today, a hundred poets will sit down
to write
knowing perfectly well
that words are only

one hand clapping
and the flesh is the other hand.

—*Siv Cedering Fox, 9/14/77*

Siv Fox is right. A hundred poets are, I am sure, thinking and writing of Robert Lowell, trying to understand and explain his life and his final offering of self without faith, the bitter "sacrament."

HOPE AMID THE DESPAIR

(*Boston Globe*, NOVEMBER 6, 1984)

After an absence of nearly two weeks, I returned to my house in Rappahannock County in mid-May of last spring. I was apprehensive that I might have missed the best part of the month.

I found that I had missed some things. The apple blossoms evidently had come and gone while I was absent, for the trees were now in green leaf. There was no sign of redbud at the edge of the woods, or of wild cherry. The dogwood was still in bloom, however. Golden ragweed was thick in the pastures, as were the buttercups.

I found the wild azaleas blooming where they should have been, along Route 618. The grass in the pastures was nearly as high as the knees of the cows. It hid the spring calves. The hay in the meadows was ready for cutting. Goatsbeard and wild phlox and sweet cicely and poppies bloomed at roadside. A few May-apple blossoms still clung to the stems beneath the umbrella leaves.

So encouraged, I bought tomato plants at Burke's store when I went to the post office to pick up my accumulated mail.

I decided to check through the mail before planting the tomatoes. I was in for a shock. There was no springlike optimism, not even hope, in my mail. Evidently the prophets of gloom, the managers of direct-mail programs, know not how the seasons run.

First, I opened a letter from the American Sentinel, warning me that American children are being brainwashed and that unless the process is stopped, and our nuclear-arms buildup continued, we and the children may eventually be destroyed by Soviet nuclear weapons. Offsetting this letter was one from the Community for Creative Non-Violence, suggesting that the only way we can escape nuclear destruction is to stop building nuclear arms.

Next I read an appeal, endorsed by Katharine Hepburn, asking for financial and moral support of population control, in some form or other, and restating the Malthusian theory that the world would be destroyed by excessive numbers of people unless action was taken now. Countering this appeal was one from the Right-to-Life organization asserting that population control will destroy civilization. No choices were being offered. I felt trapped.

There was a letter from the Committee to Re-elect Ronald Reagan, which made dire predictions of things to come if he were not reelected. And set against this was a letter from the chairman of the Democratic party telling me that he thought I would "agree with him" that the reelection of Ronald Reagan might be disastrous for the nation, if not the world.

There was a letter from James Watt, former secretary of the interior, telling me that President Reagan was a voice in the "wilderness," which critics of Watt and Reagan said was about to be destroyed.

The Watt appeal for support in subduing the wilderness was countered by a circular from *National Geographic*, which urged me to buy a book entitled *Our Threatened Inheritance.*

Then there were three letters telling me that I could and should not trust the press, generally, but that the publications recommended for subscription in the letters were reliable.

There was an appeal from the American Heart Association asking for contributions to support research in heart diseases, the "greatest man-killer."

At that point, near despair, I was distracted by the sound of an automobile horn, and by the barking of my dog.

When I went out of the house to investigate, I found that a large green Cadillac, of some years' service, had been driven into my driveway. I thought it might be a bottled-gas salesman, or possibly someone intent on selling me a water-softener system.

It was not. It was a Jehovah's Witness, who had come over the Blue Ridge Mountains from Luray to warn the people of Rappahannock County of the signs and portents of destruction, of Armageddon, and of the coming of the Kingdom.

I listened to his message, to his quotations from the Bible, with rising optimism. I told him of the depressing mail I had just gone through and of how his words had uplifted my spirit. He looked a little puzzled. I bought three pamphlets from him, and told him that with the hope and trust that his message had revived, I was going to plant tomatoes, hoping for, at least, one more crop.

I did the planting, and last week picked the last of what was a very good crop.

INDEX